GV
889
F84

Fuller, Bob, 1939-

Basketball's
wishbone offense

23744 -2

DATE			
MAR 9			
OCT 1 0 1994			
Nov 11 94			
FEB 08 '95			
MAY 0 6 '95			
JUN 2 9 2004			

Basketball's Wishbone Offense

Basketball's Wishbone Offense

BOB FULLER

Parker Publishing Company, Inc.
West Nyack, New York

© 1973, by

Parker Publishing Company, Inc.
West Nyack, New York

Library of Congress Cataloging in Publication Data

Fuller, Bob.
    Basketball's wishbone offense.

    1. Basketball—Offense.   I. Title.
GV889.F84   796.32'32   73-16034
ISBN 0-13-056424-9

Printed in the United States of America

Dedication

- *To my wife Cheryl and daughter Wendy, the coach's perfect assistants*

- *To my mother, who "showed me the way" through trying times*

- *To all my present and former ballplayers for their many sacrifices*

- *To my present and former assistant coaches, especially Dave Fultz, Jim Swift, and Tom Green, whose loyalty and dedication have been deeply appreciated*

Foreword

Winning basketball games isn't just a job for Bob Fuller, it's a science. In just ten years of varsity coaching, Fuller has compiled an almost unbelievable record of 220-57. That is an average per year of 22 wins and less than six losses. Last season, Fuller took his St. Edward (Elgin) team to the Illinois State Tournament, capturing the school's first Regional, Sectional and Super-Sectional Championships and advancing to the final five before losing on a last-second shot. St. Edward compiled a 25-3 record, best in the school's history, and won their first Suburban Catholic Western Conference title.

One year prior to Fuller's arrival the school won just one game all year. Fuller accomplished this amazing record with only one starter over six-feet tall. In fact, Fuller has never had a tall team in his ten years of coaching. His center at St. Edward at 6'4" is the tallest man he's ever coached; yet Fuller is a consistent winner. His teams have won six conference and eleven tournament championships in just ten seasons. Fuller does it with an offense he calls the "Wishbone," a tenacious defense and uncanny free-throw shooting (77% in 1972).

Well-liked and well-respected in his profession, Fuller describes his Wishbone offense in detail in this book and also tells how a coach can turn free-throw shooting and a bowl of fruit (the banana series) into victory after victory.

Bill Kindt
Sports Editor (Assistant)
Elgin Courier News
Elgin, Illinois

Acknowledgments

A couple of play patterns from the Wishbone, including the baseline-series action, are very similar to the "V" Offense options used with much success by Valparaiso, Indiana High School's Virgil Sweet. Coach Sweet has won 13 sectional championships (in his 18-year tenure) where the school had won only 1 in 23 previously. One of the leading coaches and gentlemen in the sport, Coach Sweet is a noted lecturer, having lectured at basketball clinics in 17 states and in Canada.

In Chapter 1 a few of the ball-handling drills incorporated into the "St. Edward Eleven" were picked up at a coaching clinic conducted by George King, athletic director at Purdue University. Coach King, an ex-N.B.A. player, was an outstanding coach at Purdue before retiring to become athletic director.

What This Book Will Show You

We developed the Wishbone Offense several years ago because the so-called conventional patterns were not working for us—due to limited talent, lack of height and lack of outstanding shooters from 15 feet or more. The Wishbone Offense has been good to us and I firmly believe it can be used with success at any level of basketball. It is a disciplined offense, yet with flexible ingredients, that have proven exciting and successful, if not frustrating to our opponents.

The main portions of the book will be the details of our tested and proven Wishbone offense. This will introduce to coaches a new offense that has been specially geared to small teams without the tall, talented players, but it can also work quite effectively with taller players. The Wishbone gets its name from the placement of the players on the floor and its resemblence to a wishbone. The Wishbone operates against man-to-man, zones or the various stunting combinations of defenses with no problem; it is the same against any defense. Regardless of your personnel you will find an option that will mean more victories for you.

Our staff feels that the time has arrived when coaches must organize an offense that suits their material and one that can operate against a man-to-man, zone and combination defenses. It is not unusual to find teams changing their defense at each time out or after a made free throw. Continually calling a time out to change the offense or shouting from the bench only tends to confuse your players. Every coach should develop an offensive system and stick with it. Minor changes should be made from year to year to fit the personnel but, basically, the pattern of play should be the same regardless of the personnel. Our play is a little unorthodox on both offense and defense so as to make our opponents play a little differently.

We believe that the key to our success is to control the tempo of the game. A one-speed team will not win consistently;

therefore, we use three tempos:

1. *Fast* . . . when we have the fast-break opportunity.
2. *Controlled* . . . our regular offensive patterns (Wishbone Offense) when we do not have the break and we go into pattern.
3. *Ball Control* . . . we go into our ball-control Wishbone when we feel we must to upset our opponent.

We feel we must take away the initiative from the opponent so that *they must adjust to our style*.

Also listed in this book is our format to improve your players through a systematic method of improving their field-goal and free-throw percentages. Our teams have a composite average over the past seven seasons of over 45% from the field. This average is even more significant when you take into consideration that small teams usually do not get a high percentage of close-in baskets. Our teams have averaged over 70% on free throws in ten seasons, winning 89 games when we did not outscore the opponent from the field. This book can raise your team's free-throw and field-goal percentages and this means more victories for you.

When you are not blessed with the big men and you have to work with average ballplayers, you have a big job ahead of you. Our motto has been "the difficult takes time, the impossible a little longer." Given a group of boys who have the ability and desire to learn, a coach's job is to develop them into a winning and maybe a championship team. We have been helped to achieve this goal by following the techniques described in this book.

Bob Fuller

Contents

Basketball's Wishbone Offense

1.

Selecting Personnel for Basketball's Wishbone Offense

Origin of the Wishbone

Seven conference titles (at four different high schools) and thirteen tournament championships in eleven years of coaching—that's what the Wishbone Offense has helped do for our teams. I have always been "blessed" with small players. The tallest team I coached averaged 5'11" in height, and the tallest player I coached stood 6'4". This was in competition in which most opponents had the 6'5"-or-over player. Also, it has been my misfortune never to have coached a boy who has gone on to be a major-college basketball player. While many prep coaches can boast of having as many as two or three boys going on to the collegiate ranks per season, I have never been so lucky.

As a result, I had to devise an offense to compensate for lack of height plus an offense for the average or "marginal" players. Several years ago, in my first coaching position, I decided to try to compose such an offense, plus an offense that could operate against all types of defenses (See Photo 1-1).

Our most recent team at St. Edward High School in Elgin, Illinois, which made it to the finals of the State Tournament at Champaign, had a "lilliputian" starting lineup of 6'4" Carroll Alters at center (or 5'11" Denny Butzow), 5'10" Craig Hedley and 5'11" Jeff Nolan at forwards, and a pair of 5'9" guards in Chris

Photo 1-1

Dolan and Bob Sauceda. No opponent on our 28-game slate had a smaller starting five. Using the Wishbone exclusively, we posted a 25-3 record, out-rebounded a majority of opponents, shot 46% from the field and 76% from the charity stripe. Much emphasis is put on field-goal and free-throw shooting by our coaching staff. We firmly believe that shooting *Can* be taught. (Our shooting programs will be explained in detail in Chapters 9 and 10.)

Our Success with the Wishbone

While in my first coaching position, after many long hours of research, scouting and talking with other coaches, I devised the Wishbone Offense. The Wishbone is a disciplined-type offense, yet with flexible ingredients, which has proven successful to me in three high schools over a ten-year period. It gets its name from the placement of players on the floor and its resemblance to the shape of a wishbone. (See Diagram 1-1.)

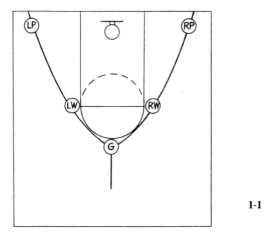

1-1

I firmly believe that this offense can be used with success at any level of basketball. I have seen the Wishbone work with winning results at the grade school, junior high, high school, independent recreational, and semi-pro levels. As an added sidelight, during a recent season, teams coached by two of my former assistants, Dave Fultz of Shabbona High School and Gary Croegaert of Amboy High School, along with our Elgin team, made it to the final 64 teams (original field, 479) in the Illinois State Tournament. All three schools used the Wishbone and had a combined won-loss record of 73-7. Ironically, Shabbona eliminated Amboy in double overtime to advance to the "Sweet 16," where we eliminated Shabbona in overtime to advance to the "Elite 8" at Champaign.

To trace some of the recent successes of our Wishbone:

A few years ago, I served as player-coach of an East Chicago, Indiana semi-pro team, which used the Wishbone in winning two league championships and five tournament championships, while posting a perfect 31-0 mark.

Later, I became athletic director and varsity basketball coach at Shabbona, Illinois High School. Shabbona had won only one conference title since the late 1950's and had obviously fallen on some hard times. Together with my assistants, Dave Fultz and Jim Swift, we installed the Wishbone with amazing results. In three years at Shabbona, we won the conference title all three seasons, winning 26 conference games in 27 attempts. In the 49-year history of the Little Ten Conference prior to our arrival, Shabbona had won only four titles. On our winning teams, the tallest player was 6'3" and our tallest team averaged just 5'11".

Recently, assistant coach Jim Swift and I left Shabbona looking for a new "challenge." We found the "challenge" at Elgin, Illinois, St. Edward High School, which had never won a West Suburban Catholic Conference championship, its highest finish being fifth. The previous year showed a 2-22 record. We installed the Wishbone at St. Edward and in our first year we finished 15-9, including an unprecedented third place conference finish. The next season, we won the coveted conference crown on the way to a 25-3 record and a place in the cherished state finals.

In a five-year period at the high-school level, the Wishbone had helped win four conference titles with an overall 115-24 won-loss record. This was accomplished, as stated before, with shortages in height and talent.

I might add that in all three schools, although height and talent might have been limited, I was blessed with kids with extreme dedication and desire, which helped to make up for other shortcomings.

Player Position Requirements

The following are the "ideal" requirements for personnel in operating the Wishbone Offense:

1. *Lonesome Guard* . . . the pointman on offense (See Diagram 1-1), should be able to drive right or left and reverse dribble with ease. He should be a 40-plus percentage shooter from the key area. Passing ability is very important, as he has to "thread the needle" often. He has the key defensive responsibilities . . . the quarterback and team leader . . . normally the best dribbler . . . Ideally, the lonesome guard's range in height should be 5'8" and up. The tallest player to have played the point for us was 5'10".

2. *Right and Left Wingmen* (See Diagram 1-1) must be able to drive, pass and shoot well. The wings are secondary re-

bounders most of the time and have responsibility of rotation for defensive floor balance. They also have weakside re bounding duties on some occasions. Normally, they are good ball handlers, better-than-average shooters, and good enough as outside shooters to keep the defense honest. Ideally, the wingmen should be 6'2" or taller. The tallest player we ever had at the wing position was 5'11"!

3. *Postmen* are the primary rebounders. They should be good spot shooters from corners . . . must be taught to take baseline on drive (and also defense!) and develop ability to crash boards at proper time . . . must be able to board well and have a hook and turn-around jumper . . . normally the tallest and strongest boys . . . should have good, quick, inside moves . . . your best inside shooters . . . Ideally, the postmen should be 6'3" or more. We have had players 5'8", 5'9", and 5'11" play entire seasons at these positions! The tallest player we ever had playing the post was 6'4". (See Diagram 1-1).

Wishbone Offense Derivatives

Every phase of our offense evolves from the regular Wishbone Offense play pattern, as shown in Diagram 1-1.

In Diagram 1-2, the arrows illustrate the movement of the players in reverting to the "Banana," or ball-control phase of the Wishbone. The Banana has proven very effective for us over the years and we have been known to play entire games using only the Banana Series play patterns. The ball-control phase will be covered in detail in Chapter 4.

Diagram 1-3 depicts our Isolation pattern, which has also proven to work very effectively for us. The Isolation play pattern will be covered in detail in Chapter 5. The arrows show our transition from the Wishbone.

Diagram 1-4 shows our Green pattern, which will be detailed in Chapter 5. The arrows show our transition from the Wishbone to the Green Play pattern.

These three illustrations represent just a few of the many

variations that may evolve from the regular Wishbone Offense play pattern.

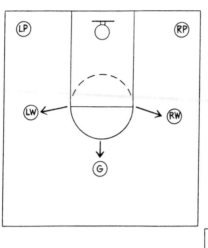

1-2

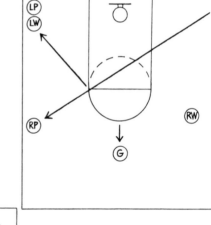

1-3

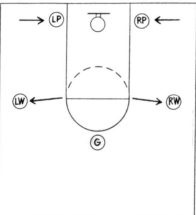

1-4

Our Favorite Pre-Season Fundamental Drills

Following are our favorite pre-season fundamental drills, which are used to complement the Wishbone Offense. It must be noted that a few of the drills listed here are also used at various times throughout the season. We use many more pre-season drills, but we have listed only our favorites in this section.

11-MAN DRILL

Diagram 1-5 illustrates our 11-man drill, which we run every day at the start of practice. This drill is of the continuity type, that is, it may continue up and down the floor until you call it to a halt. The drill involves every fundamental in the book—including the passing, timing, shooting, running and dribbling phases of the game.

If you have more than 11 boys on your squad, you can alternate the players. Sometimes we replace one or more of the 11

1-5

boys on the floor with an extra boy when they commit errors, fail to hustle, etc.

In the 11-man drill, 1, 2 and 3 take the ball down the floor (1 has the ball). X1 and X2 are in the tandem defense for the fast break. X1 challenges the ball, X2 takes the first pass and X1 drops off to the opposite side. When the shot is taken, 1, 2 and 3, and X1 and X2 are rebounders. The player who gets the rebound throws out to the side (outlet men) to 4 and 5. For example, if X2 rebounds he joins 4 and 5 in moving to the opposite end of the floor.

X1 and 1, 2 and 3 fill in the remaining positions—two as the outlet rebound men and two in the defensive tandem. The drill continues up and down the floor until you call it to a halt.

RUN-THE-LINES DRILL

We usually use this drill at the close of practice. The players line up, arm's length apart on the endline. On signal, the players go full steam to the parallel of the first free-throw line. They touch the floor, then return to the original station. They then run to the midcourt line and return; then to the free throw line at the opposite end of the court and return; and finally to the endline at the opposite end and return. The four steps are executed continuously and at full speed. As many repetitions as desired may be run.

We sometimes place a time limit (30 seconds or under) to complete the whole cycle. As other alternatives, you may have the players dribble the lines or run the lines backwards.

ONE-ON-ONE, FULL-COURT DRILL (Diagram 1-6)

This drill is a great conditioner; it helps to develop good one-on-one moves, defense, and brings out "pride" in an individual. We like to run this drill as a "tournament," with players' names being drawn out of a hat in random order. This always creates intense interest, as each boy strives to become the team's one-on-one champion.

The coach throws the ball up against the backboard from the mid-court area as both boys break for the ball. The boy who gets the ball becomes the offensive player and goes for the opposite basket. The drill goes full court with no boundary lines.

One point is given for a steal, two points for a basket and a one-and-bonus free throw for each foul. The winner is the first player to reach a combination of six points. If the offensive player can retrieve his own shot, he can go back to the other basket and score.

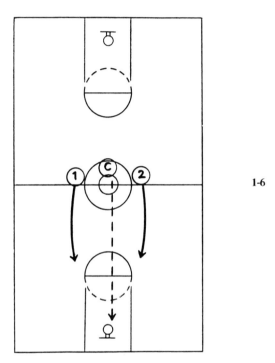

1-6

OUR STATION DRILLS

Our station drills are illustrated in Diagram 1-7.

Station 1 is our wall-tipping area. Each player takes a basketball and, without looking, dribbles the ball against the wall using only his fingertips. This is a one-minute drill that helps develop touch and tingertip control.

Station 2 is our rope-jumping area. Rope jumping helps improve leg strength, timing and coordination. Count the number of jumps each player can do in one minute.

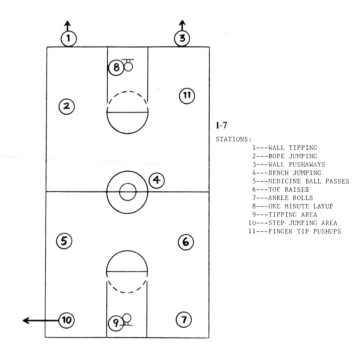

1-7

STATIONS:

1---WALL TIPPING
2---ROPE JUMPING
3---WALL PUSHAWAYS
4---BENCH JUMPING
5---MEDICINE BALL PASSES
6---TOE RAISES
7---ANKLE ROLLS
8---ONE MINUTE LAYUP
9---TIPPING AREA
10---STEP JUMPING AREA
11---FINGER TIP PUSHUPS

Station 3 is our wall-pushaway area. The player stands facing the wall with both arms extended out in front toward a wall. He points his fingers up so that the palms of the hands face the wall. Keeping his body straight and without moving his feet, the player slowly allows himself to fall forward, stopping himself using his extended hands. The player should not bend his elbows. After falling, he pushes himself back to an upright position by pushing with his fingers on the wall. The player should then snap his hands downward at the wrists as his fingers leave the wall. Record how many repetitions each boy can do in one minute.

Station 4 is for bench jumping. Using a regular dressing room bench or a board secured between two folding chairs, have the boys stand with their sides to the bench, about six inches away from it. Players should have their arms and knees bent. They jump sideward and over the bench. As soon as they hit the floor on the other side of the bench, they immediately jump back over the bench to the original position. Record how many jumps each boy can do in a one-minute period. An outstanding jumper can do about one per second. In the early season, you should start with

30-second periods and increase the duration of the exercise daily.

Station 5 is for medicine-ball passes. The boys pair off and see how many passes they can make in a one-minute period. The boys use overhead and two-hand chest passes.

Station 6 is our toe-raisers area. The boys raise up on their toes from a flat footed position. Again, they should record the number they can do in one minute.

Station 7 is our ankle-roll area. The boys walk on the sides of their ankles, in and out, and record the number they can do in one minute.

Station 8 is our one-minute layup area. The player shoots a layup from one side of the basket and then the other, without allowing the ball to touch the floor. The player should record the number of baskets he can make in one minute.

Station 9 is our tipping area. The player throws the ball against the backboard, then jumps high in the air and tips it in approximately the same spot, then jumps and tips again and again. The boys should record how many consecutive times they can tip the ball in one minute.

Station 10 is our fingertip-pushup area. The boys record how many fingertip pushups they can do in one minute.

Station 11 is our step-jumping area. The boys use a flight of stairs, starting at the bottom and balancing on one foot. They jump up to the next step, taking off and landing on the same foot, until they have gone about ten steps. Thev should walk back down and then go up using the other leg.

The boys move from one station to another, in one-minute intervals, on the coach's whistle.

ST. EDWARD ELEVEN

The St. Edward Eleven is a series of ball-handling drills that we use five to eight minutes daily, especially in the early season. Besides helping our ball clubs fundamentally we find that the drills improve hand-to-eye coordination and hand and finger strength. A player should work for speed and rhythm.

Several of the following drills were picked up at a clinic featuring George King, athletic director and former basketball coach at Purdue University.

1. Right leg circle—left leg circle

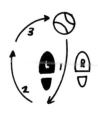

The player should assume a semi-crouched position with ball in front of body at knee level. The feet should be spread at shoulder width. The player circles one leg at a time with the ball. Ball starts in right hand in front of body and player brings the ball around left leg to front position into right hand. Continue this movement around one leg, then stop and start around the other leg, starting movement with left hand passing ball back between legs, circling right leg.

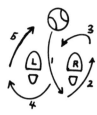

2. Figure eight

The player assumes same position as in Number One. Keep the ball in left hand and put it between legs where the right hand receives the ball. The right hand then passes ball around right leg and back through legs to left hand.

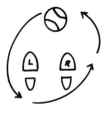

3. Around the body

Same position as in Number One. Carry ball around left side with left hand to right hand and around to front again. Change directions at any time. Start with the ball around the waist, then move it down around knees, and then around ankles. Go up and down in this fashion.

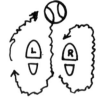

4. Figure-eight dribble

Same position as in Number One. Follow the same pattern as in Number Two, only this time dribble, keeping the ball low.

5. Figure eight with drop

Use same body position as in Number One. Start this exercise as a regular Figure Eight but, when bringing ball around left leg with left hand, do not put ball between legs. Swing it on around in front to right, which then carries ball around right leg through legs from back side. Bring ball to left hand, then, merely drop ball to court, and quickly exchange hand positions by bringing right arm around in front and putting left arm to rear. Grasp ball with both hands as it bounces up and continue maneuver.

6. Up and down the body using fingertips

Keep body erect with ball out in front of body at arms' length. Keep elbows locked. Tap ball from one hand to other while moving the ball above head and down to knees in a gradual movement. When controlling ball over head, shuffle feet from side to side.

7. Crab run

Assume a crouched running position and start an exaggerated long-stride run. As you step out with left leg, place ball under that thigh with right hand to left hand movement. Then as right leg comes up and forward, use a left-hand-to-right movement, passing ball under right thigh. Continue on down court as fast as you can with this drill. Ball makes same movement as in stationary figure-eight drill.

8. Spin ball on finger and "pop" the ball

The player stands erect and spins the ball on the end of his finger. We have had players spin the ball in and out of the legs on one finger in a figure-eight drill. By popping the ball we mean slapping the ball from one hand to the other. This will develop hand and finger strength.

9. Bounce ball back to front and catch

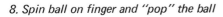

Same starting position as in Number Eight. The player holds ball in both hands behind back and bounces ball between legs and catches ball in front.

10. Bounce ball front to back and catch

Same starting position as in Number Eight. The player holds ball in both hands in front of body and then bounces ball between legs and catches ball behind back.

11. Toss ball behind back and catch

Same starting position as in Number eight. The player tosses ball over his head and catches ball behind his back with both hands.

Wishbone Versatility

To me the real beauty of the Wishbone is its versatility. In preparation for our opponents we simply modify our Wishbone options to meet a certain defense instead of being forced to spend extra and precious practice time on an entirely new offense for each opponent we face.

We have unwavered confidence in the Wishbone and we are certain that it affords us scoring opportunities that aren't available with other types of offenses.

I am not saying that the Wishbone is infallible, nor am I guaranteeing you a victory against every team you play. However, I will guarantee you that when the Wishbone is executed properly, your team will get the good scoring options that are hard to come by when using other types of offenses. I can't remember being defeated in many games in which I could blame the Wishbone or our opponent's defense in halting the Wishbone.

Salient Points of the Wishbone

The following are some of the salient points of the Wishbone Offense:

1. It spreads the defense, allowing teams with good ball handlers to drive the middle.
2. A one-point offense does not permit a pressure-type defense to double-team or overload very well.

3. Good defensive balance and excellent rebounding position on the offensive board are always available. There are always one and one-half rebounders on the weak side.
4. It keeps the defense occupied on the ball and away from the ball. It should force the defensive man to turn his back.
5. It provides defensive balance by rotating the guard and the weak-side wingman.
6. The offense is the same against zone, man-to-man and combinations.
7. Because of the "lonesome guard," you may play one guard and four "big" players if you so desire.
8. All options end with the baseline series, which gives the offense continuity.
9. The offense can be operated on either side of the floor with the same movements or options.
10. It is not a tiring offense and its simple patterns are easy to understand. It is uncomplicated.
11. It is impossible to keep this offense from getting a good shot if it is timed and executed properly.

2.

Setting Up Basketball's
Wishbone Offense

Did you hear the one about the head basketball coach who ran into his assistant on the way to the gym and immediately started to babble:

Wow, did I have a terrific dream last night. I dreamt I met a beautiful blonde with a 38-22-38 figure, who grabbed me by the arm, told me she had always admired me, and then insisted upon taking me up to her room . . . where she introduced me to her 7-foot kid brother!!

Coach, perhaps you are one of the thousands of coaches in the country who has dreams but still must go out each week on the court with the little guys. I never coached a team that averaged over six feet in height and the tallest high school player I ever coached stood just 6'4". As a result, we had to devise an offense to compensate for lack of height, plus an offense for the "average" player. When you don't have the "horses," meaning tall and talented ball players, you must improvise and adjust and stress the specifics to your players in order to be successful.

Signals for the Wishbone

Both audible and visual signals can be used by players to

regulate the type of play pattern to be used. An audible signal is usually the calling of the name or number of the alignment or play pattern. Some coaches permit the guard to determine the pattern by means of a hand signal as he dribbles down court.

A visual key, which is what we use, is given by a hand (finger) signal. Thus, if we are in the Give and Go Screen play pattern of our offense, the player can signal either by barking out "two" or by signaling with two fingers held high in the air. We have either of the two wingmen designated to give the signal.

Placement of Players

The offense derives its name from the placement of players on the floor and its resemblance to a wishbone, which was adopted officially as the name of the offense. Diagram 1-1 shows the basic alignment for the wishbone regardless of the play pattern. All the play patterns and variations of this offense, such as the banana, isolation, etc., evolve off this basic alignment.

For example, if the wishbone is in the banana (ball control—Chapter 4), the wingman and guard move further out on the court. The guard starts the offense at the top of the key approximately 21 to 23 feet from the endline, as in Diagram 2-1. The rightwing and leftwing can be wide or tight approximately 19 feet from the endline. The rightpost and leftpost are half-way to the corners about 5 feet from the endline. The players are constantly moving and exchange positions as the ball moves from one side of the court to the other.

For example, when the ball goes down the right side of the court, the rightpost would extend further to the corner and the leftpost would move into closer rebound position on the weak side. The weak-side wingman (leftwing) would move down toward the endline, trying to occupy his man or the man in his area and at the same time moving into a closer rebound position if a shot is taken from the right side of the floor. This actually gives you one and one-half rebounders on the weak side.

For purposes of simplicity, all play patterns in this book will originate on the right side of the floor. All play patterns can be run to either side of the floor with the same continuity.

As shown in Diagram 2-2, the leftwing is also ready, if the play is stopped on the right side, to sprint back to the head of the key area to bring the ball back around to the weak side and to initiate the baseline series, which will be explained in detail later in this chapter.

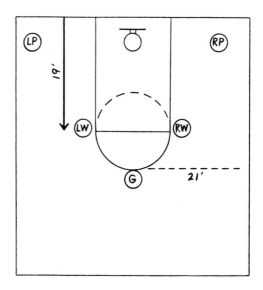

2-1

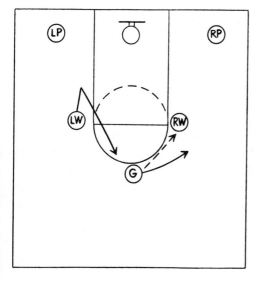

2-2

Wingman Cutback—Play Pattern #1

This is the easiest play pattern to teach on the Wishbone. It also goes into the baseline series quicker than any other pattern. In Diagram 2-3, the rightwing has faked down and cut back to receive the pass from the guard. The leftpost has "cheated in" towards the basket. The rightpost has moved deep into the corner.

The leftwing has faked his man down towards the basket, trying to get him to turn his back on the basket. Then the leftwing fakes, using a jab step, and cuts back hard toward the strong side of the court to receive a pass from the rightwing. If the rightwing cannot hit the leftwing, his next option would be to shoot if open, or he could drive for the basket, since the strong side of the floor is open, as the leftwing clears to the weak side of the floor.

In Diagram 2-4, the rightwing returns the ball to the guard as the play is stopped on the strong side. The rightwing was unable to pass, shoot or drive. The leftpost moves into the left free-throw line parallel in front of the leftwing, facing the ball with his left foot on the first hash mark approximately 4 feet from the basket and 8 feet from the endline. The guard now dribbles to his left to initiate the baseline series continuity, which is the finale of all the regular play patterns. The play pattern, as in all the other Wishbone options, can be run to either side of the floor with equal effectiveness.

An ideal team would be one that could run each of the play patterns in this book with equal effectiveness. Usually, you will find one or two patterns and run them most of the time. As an example, in our upset of Aurora Marmion recently, we used one simple pattern in the third quarter to jump from a tie to a 10-point lead. We used the wingman cutback versus Aurora's 3-2 zone for four straight baskets. Aurora called time out and switched to a tight man-to-man. We ran the same pattern three more times and garnered three more baskets! These seven consecutive baskets with the wingman cutback play pattern, versus both man-to-man and zone defenses, were highly instrumental in our narrow 58 to 56 win.

We will now discuss the final phase of all our play patterns: the continuous baseline series.

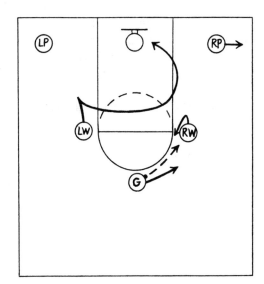

2-3

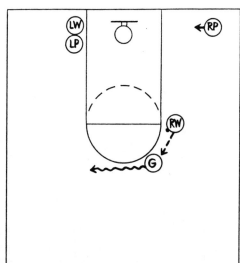

2-4

Baseline Series—The Finale of All Regular Patterns

In the following patterns in this chapter and in Chapter 3, each play pattern will end in the baseline series. The reader can check back to this section for the proper baseline series execution.

We will use the Wingman Cutback Play Pattern #1 example. However, any of the five offensive men may be in any of the offensive patterns on the baseline series. The individual positioning of the feet of the five offensive men would be arranged as shown in Diagram 2-5.

In Diagram 2-7, the guard dribbles over and hits the leftwing, who has sprinted towards the left corner. The leftwing delays and times his cut to the corner after the guard has initiated the play by taking a dribble to the left. At the same time, the leftwing is moving towards the corner; the leftpost swings his right leg toward the baseline and begins to close out his man or the man in his area. (See Diagram 2-6 for the foot positions of the leftpost in closing out.)

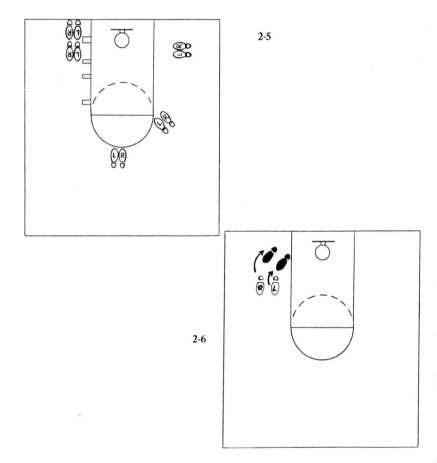

2-5

2-6

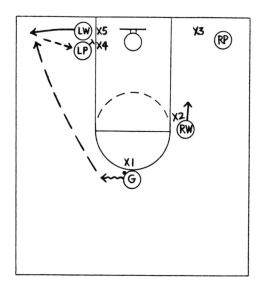

2-7

If the leftwing is open (and often he will be) he can shoot a jumper from the corner. By using a rocker-step, he can also fake a jumper and drive by his defensive man for a close-in shot. If the leftwing is not free, he can make two types of passes into the leftpost, who is busy closing out his defensive man. If the defensive man is overplaying the baseline side of the leftpost, the leftwing passes away from the baseline and the leftpost can shoot a close-in hook shot or a turn-around shot. If the defensive man overplays away from the baseline, the leftwing passes to the leftpost on the baseline side and the leftpost shoots a close-in layup, using his body to screen out the defensive man.

As another option (Diagram 2-8), if, after running the pattern a few times, the defensive men concentrate on the pass to the corner, often the leftpost will be left alone with no defensive man at all. The guard then passes directly to the underneath man, the leftpost. Or, the pass can go directly to the leftpost from the guard if the leftpost has his man sufficiently closed out.

Diagram 2-9 gives continuity to the baseline series as it forms an option when the leftwing or guard cannot pass into the leftpost, or when the leftwing is unable to shoot. The pass comes back out to

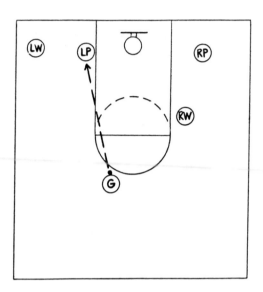

2-8

the guard who sprints over to meet the pass. The guard then hits the rightwing, who has faked down and come back to the top of the key. As this is taking place, the leftwing cuts across the baseline and lines up behind the rightpost on the right side of the floor. The rightwing, who has received the ball from the guard, now starts the baseline series by dribbling to the right. The leftwing pauses and then times his cut to the right corner when the rightwing starts to dribble. You may run this man (in this case the leftwing) on the baseline, side-to-side, as many times as you desire. This play action can be continued until a scoring option occurs or you reset and initiate another play pattern. (Diagram 2-10.)

If a coach so desires, the baseline series can become a play pattern in itself, as you could go right to the baseline series to start an option. One quick way of doing this would be to send either wing directly to the baseline behind a postman, as in Diagram 2-10. Thus, the baseline series in itself becomes a play pattern.

During a recent season, we met Newark in the game that was to decide whether or not we were to win an unprecedented third consecutive conference title. We had beaten Newark three weeks earlier, in the semifinals of a tournament, 56-55 in three overtimes. We had some trouble with Newark's 2-1-2 half-court press in this game, so our coaching staff got together to figure out some adjustments. We decided simply to go right to the baseline series, sending our wingman down the floor immediately before we approached mid-court with the ball. We jumped out to a quick 15 to 1 lead, forcing Newark to switch to a matchup zone, a 3-2 zone and, finally, a three-quarter-court 2-1-2. We held on to our early lead to win our third straight crown by a ten-point margin.

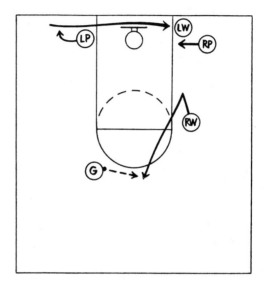

2-9

2-10

Give-and-Go Screen—Play Pattern #2

The rightwing meets the pass from the guard to start this play pattern. The rightwing's first option is to shoot or drive. If he is unable to do either, he passes to the rightpost and cuts through, looking for a return pass. The rightpost may shoot or pass off to the cutting rightwing. (Diagram 2-11.)

If none of these options is possible, the rightwing screens for the leftpost, who cuts into a low post position on the strong side. The leftpost looks for a pass from the rightpost. If he receives the pass, he shoots a turnaround shot or a hook shot. (Diagram 2-12.)

In Diagram 2-12, when the rightpost cannot pass to the leftpost, he passes quickly back to the guard. At the same time, the leftpost continues to the weak side of the floor setting up in baseline-series formation in front of the rightwing. The leftwing has faked down and come back out to the top of the key for a pass from the guard. The leftwing initiates the baseline series with a dribble to the left as the rightwing sprints to the corner and the leftpost closes out in his area. (Diagram 2-13.)

At this point, the reader should review Diagram 2-5 through 2-10 for a complete review of the scoring options of the baseline series.

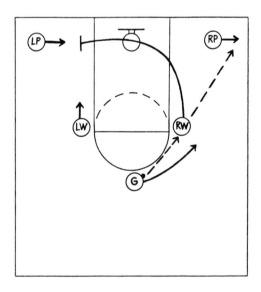

2-11

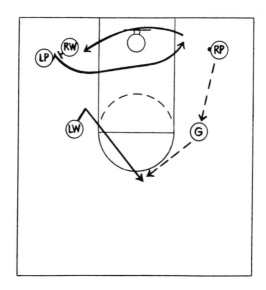

2-12

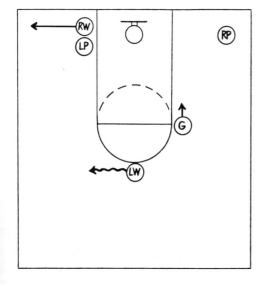

2-13

Play-Pattern Drills for the Wishbone

We use the following play-pattern drills derived from our offense, and we run the drills from both sides of the court. Other play-pattern drills will be detailed throughout the book.

WINGMAN-CUTBACK DRILLS (Diagram 2-14)

1. The coach passes to the wing, who breaks down and then back to meet the pass. The wing then looks for the opposite wing from the left side, who has faked and cut hard for the basket. The players then switch lines. No defense is used.
2. Add a token defense. This is a passive defense that merely stays with the offense. No attempt is made to intercept passes or block shots.
3. The defense goes "live" and the wing adds the drive or shoot options.
4. Run the regular play pattern with five offensive and five defensive men, against various defenses, such as man-to-man, zone, and other combinations.

BASELINE SERIES (Diagram 2-15)

1. The players use all the options in the baseline series with no defense.
2. Add a "token" defense to the wing and post but not to the guard.
3. Add a token defense to the guard also.
4. Have the defense go live.
5. Run the baseline series, five-on-five, versus the various defenses.

GIVE-AND-GO DRILLS (Diagram 2-16)

1. The wing hits the post, fakes and cuts hard for the basket. The post can pass to the wing or hit the opposite post who cuts hard off the screen by the wing.
2. Add a token defense.
3. The defense goes live and the wing and post add the drive and shoot options.
4. Run the give-and-go screen pattern, five-on-five, versus various defenses.

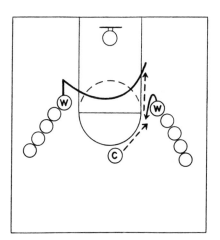

2-14

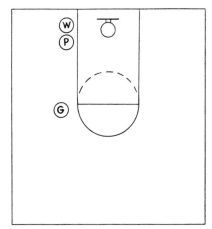

2-15

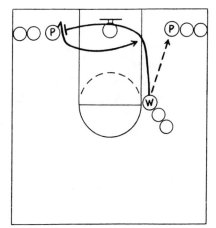

2-16

Gimmicks in Teaching the Wishbone

There is always the temptation on the part of the coach to add more play patterns to the offense before the players have mastered or successfully executed the basic patterns. A coach and his team are far better off if they can run a few basic play patterns with proper execution.

It is common knowledge among our rivals that opposing teams only have to scout our teams once. Our competitors say "They run the same options year after year." They are right! The catch here is that, so far, no defense has been able to cope with our offense consistently, if at all.

Before any worthwhile offense can be developed, basic fundamentals must be well-learned. A basketball team attempting to run an offense without sound fundamentals is akin to hunting a bear with a switch.

Following are some of our "gimmicks" in teaching the Wishbone:

1. Know the offense backwards and forwards before you try to teach it. Use the chalkboard. A portable board on the floor would be ideal.
2. Drill your squad well in fundamentals. Chapter 8 gives all of our favorite offensive drills in detail.
3. Show the entire play pattern to the team and then walk through it on the floor.
4. Use chalk or tape to diagram some of the key positions on the floor.
5. Break the offense down into parts. Go over it, option by option. It is a good idea to alternate the players at the various positions.
6. Use a passive, "token" defense in which the defensive men move with the offense, but do not attempt to interfere with passes, shots, etc.
7. Use a live defense, running at full speed.
8. Play the "Three-Mistakes Half-Court Drill" described in Chapter 4.
9. Now go full court for seven to ten minutes.

3.

Running Basketball's
Wishbone Offense

The three play sequences in this chapter—the Postman Roll, Block and Roll, and the Lonesome-Guard Reverse—are the three remaining patterns in our regular Wishbone system.

Postman Roll—Play Pattern #3

The rightwing fakes downward and then meets the pass from the lonesome guard to initiate the Postman-Roll play pattern. As shown in Diagram 3-1, the rightpost sets a screen (feet widespread and hands at side) on the rightwing's defensive man. When setting the screen, the rightpost should take up as much room as possible to the upside of the defensive man. The rightwing drives quickly over the screen using his right hand—the one away from his defensive man.

As in our other regular play patterns, the leftwing occupies his man by faking downward toward the basket, ready to rebound on the weak side or break out to the top of the key area to initiate the baseline series on a pass from the rightwing. The leftpost has "cheated in" for rebound position, occupying his man, and is also ready to go strong side off a screen by the rightpost if this option develops. As in other patterns, on all options, the men not directly

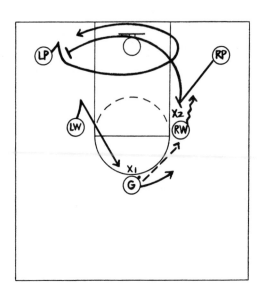

3-1

involved in the play run a two-step clearout occupying their man or the man in their area.

It is very important that good floor position is maintained by the rightpost when setting the pick. The screen must be in an area within the wing's scoring range. The rightwing's first option is to drive all the way if the path is clear. The rightwing may also shoot a jumper off the screen if he is open. As a third option, the rightwing may hit the rightpost on his roll to the basket. The rightpost does not roll immediately, but waits until he is sure that the rightwing is not going to drive or shoot.

Note: If the defense is man-to-man, the instant the rightpost sees his defensive man switching, he rolls for the basket. If the defensive man on the rightwing fights through the block over the top, it is the fault of the rightwing for not dribbling close enough to the block initially. If the rightwing's defensive man goes behind the block, it is the fault of the rightpost who has not rolled properly to screen the man with his body.

If the rightpost does not get the ball, he sets a screen on the leftpost's defensive man (or the man in the area) on the weak side of the floor. The rightpost must set a stationary wide screen on the side of the leftpost's defensive man.

Note: If, after a few times, the defense adjusts to the leftpost faking low and going high, the leftpost can fake high and break low off the screen for a possible easy layup.

If the rightwing can do none of the first three scoring options, his fourth option is to pass to the leftpost who has faked low and come off the screen by the rightpost, circling to the strong side. If the rightwing can do none of the four options, he passes back out to the guard who has sprinted to the strong side. While this is happening, the leftpost returns to the weak side and sets up in back of the rightpost. The baseline series is now initiated as the guard passes to the leftwing, who dribbles left. This is illustrated in Diagram 3-2. This play pattern, as with all other regular Wishbone options, can be run to either side of the floor with equal effectiveness.

An example of the postman-roll pattern in action is our Little Ten Conference debut versus Serena High School. Serena was the pre-season choice for the loop crown. We used the postman-roll pattern exclusively in the first quarter and scored on our first ten shots from the field. With 3:30 remaining in the first stanza, we led 21 to 0! What a way to break into a conference! We used the rest of our patterns throughout the remainder of the contest and led 42-13 at halftime. The final score was 77-38. For the game, we shot an amazing 67%, canning 32 of 48 field-goal attempts.

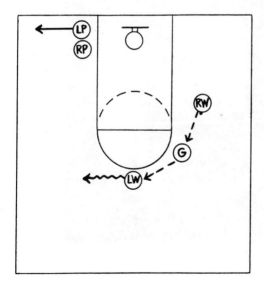

3-2

Block-and-Roll—Play Pattern #4 (See Photo 3-1)

The block-and-roll pattern has been good to us over the years
and it is often the pattern we go to when we need a quick basket.
As shown in Diagram 3-3, the rightwing sets a screen with his feet
spread wide, hands at side, on the guard's defensive man. The
guard drives up the floor and drives off the block with his right
hand. It is important that the rightwing's block be set to the right
of the key area. If the defensive man moves toward the block the
rightwing holds his position. If the defensive man tries to go
behind the screen the wingman rolls immediately screening the
defensive man with his body. The wingman rolls belly to the ball
keeping the defensive man on his back. If the defensive man goes
over the top of the block ahead of the dribbler, it is the fault of
the dribbler, in this case the guard. If the defensive man goes
behind the block to intercept the dribbler, it is the fault of the
wingman setting the block because he did not keep the defensive

Photo 3-1

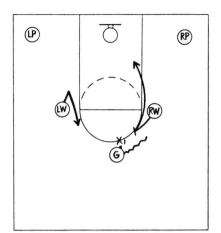

3-3

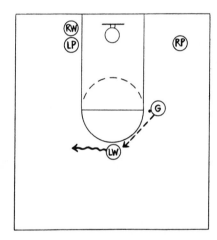

3-4

man screened with his body. As in our other regular play patterns, the men not directly involved in the play run a two-step clearout occupying their man in their area.

The guard's first option, as seen in Diagram 3-3, is to drive all the way off the block for a layup if the middle is open. The middle should be open if the rightpost pulls to the corner, occupying his man, and the leftpost and the leftwing are busy occupying their defensive men. A second option is for the guard to jump-shoot off the screen. A third option for the guard is to pass to the rightwing who is rolling, belly to ball, to the basket. If the defense switches men, the wing should be open for an easy pass as he rolls to the basket.

If the guard has none of the first three options, he picks up his dribble and passes back to the leftwing, who has faked downward and then burst out to the top of the key area to meet the guard's pass. The rightwing, who originally set the block, has now rolled through to the weak side and goes behind the leftpost to initiate the baseline series. The leftpost has moved into position from the weak side on the pass from the guard to the leftwing. (Please refer to Chapter 2 for the details of the baseline series. The player positions are illustrated in Diagram 3-4.)

Diagram 3-5 shows the option if the defense counters with the defensive postman (in this case X4) sagging into the free throw lane area to stop the drive by the guard or the roll by the wingman. We counter this by having the guard immediately passing to the rightpost. The rightwing who set the screen immediately rolls to the strongside of the lane looking for a quick return pass from the rightpost. Sometimes this pass can be made for an easy basket, but usually the rightwing will set up in the low-post area, where, if he can close out his man, he is in position to receive a pass for an easy close-in basket. The rightpost can also shoot if he cannot get the ball into the rightwing. If the rightpost cannot shoot or pass to the rightwing, he immediately passes back

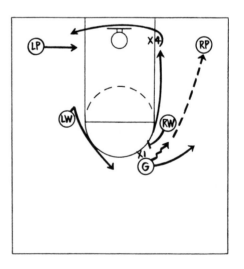

3-5

to the guard who has moved over on the first pass. The guard then passes to the leftwing, who has faked downward and busted out to the top of the key area. The baseline series takes place as the leftpost takes position and the rightwing rolls through to the weak side directly behind the leftpost. The leftwing initiates the baseline series with a couple of dribbles to the left.

If the defense counters with the defensive wingman moving out side or a jump-switch between the guard and wing, the offense can counter with the following, which has proved effective for us. (Diagram 3-6 depicts this option.)

When the guard sees the switch he immediately picks up the ball. The rightwing, also noticing the switch, delays and does not roll to the basket. The leftwing, who has faked his man downward towards the basket, now uses a jab step (as in the wingman-cut-back pattern) and cuts to the strong side of the lane, looking for a pass from the guard. As an alternative, the guard can pass to the rightpost who can then pass into the leftwing. If the guard or rightpost cannot pass to the rolling leftwing the pass comes back to the guard, who passes back to the rightwing, who dribbles left to initiate the baseline series. The rightwing, who originally set the screen, has rolled back to the top of the key area. The leftwing cuts through to the weak side setting up in front of the leftpost, who has moved in from the corner. (Diagram 3-7.)

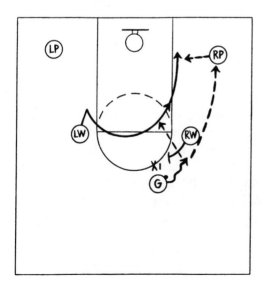

3-6

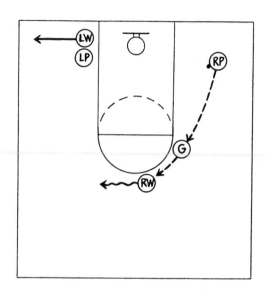

3-7

Lonesome-Guard Reverse—Play Pattern #5

Diagram 3-8 shows our lonesome-guard reverse pattern in which we send our guard directly to the baseline on the strong side to initiate what appears to be the baseline series. If there is no play, we reverse the action to the weak side with the postman setting a high screen on the wingman. If no play develops on this option, the ball is reversed again as the baseline series develops on the opposite (or original) side.

For example, in Diagram 3-8, the Lonesome guard passes to the rightwing who has faked downward and back to meet the pass. The rightwing's first option is to shoot or drive if open. We rarely have this option. The rightwing's second option is to pass back to the guard who is busting hard down the middle. The rightwing's third option is to pass back to the guard who is coming off of the rightpost's screen. An alternate move would be for the rightwing to pass into the rightpost, who has turned facing the ball after setting the screen and is now closing out the man in his area. It should be noted that on a shot by the guard, the rightwing also has rebound responsibilities.

If the guard cannot shoot or pass under to the rightpost he immediately reverses action by passing back to the rightwing. (See

Diagram 3-9.) After passing, the guard sprints back to the right-side area. The rightwing then passes back to the leftwing, who has faked downward and sprinted back to the top of the key area. The leftpost comes up high to set a screen on the leftwing's defensive man. The leftwing has the option of driving all the way for the layup, shooting off the block, or passing to the leftpost

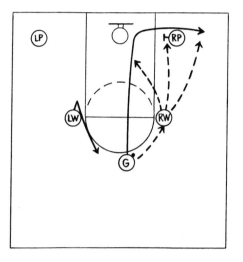

3-8

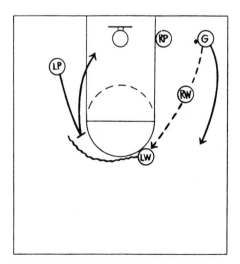

3-9

who is rolling for the basket. The same blocking rules apply here as in the other play patterns.

If the leftwing has none of the options open, he reverses the action to the weak side by passing back to the guard. The guard passes to the rightwing, who has faked to meet the pass. The rightwing takes one or two dribbles to the right to initiate the baseline series with the leftpost breaking to the corner after setting up behind the rightpost. This is depicted in Diagram 3-10.

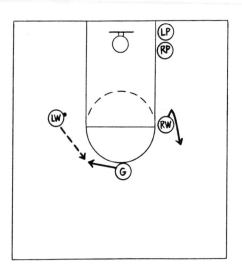

3-10

Examples of the Wishbone
Versus Zone Defenses

As stated in the opening chapter, the five regular Wishbone patterns described in Chapter 2 and the first sections of this chapter work equally well against man-to-man and zone defenses. Naturally, certain play patterns will work more effectively against a certain type of zone than others. Also, different patterns will work better for certain teams than they will for others. For example, the wingman-cutback pattern has always worked better for us versus a 1-2-2 zone than it has against other defenses. However, any of the play patterns will work against any type of zone, especially if run all the way through to the baseline series.

For the sake of brevity, in this section we will show one play pattern against a certain zone. We will use the standard zones: the

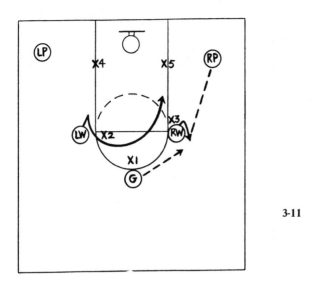

3-11

1-2-2; 2-1-2; 1-3-1; 3-2; 2-3; and 2-2-1. Examples of our five regular play patterns versus the combination defenses, matchup defenses, etc., will be illustrated in Chapter 7. Diagram 3-11 shows an example of the wingman-cutback pattern against a zone defense. The wingman-cutback, just as all Wishbone play patterns, will work against any type of zone. Here, we will show the pattern versus a 1-2-2 zone.

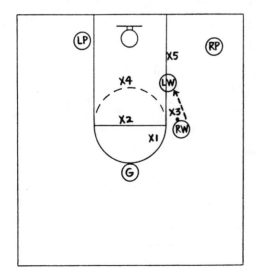

3-12

3-13

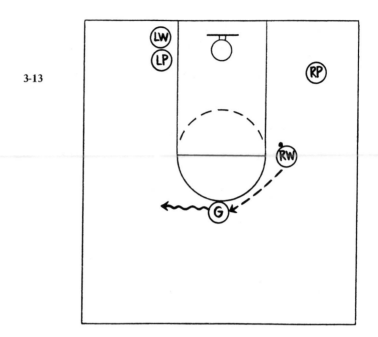

3-14

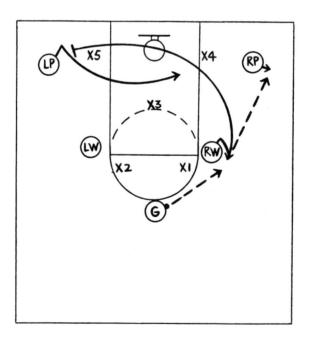

As depicted in Diagram 3-11, while using the wingman-cutback, if X5 shifts properly, the leftwing, on his cut down the lane, could be open for a layup or a short turn-around shot in the lane. The leftwing should pick his spot or opening in the zone. Another option would be for the rightwing to pass to the rightpost for a quick corner shot if X5 sags in the lane, or, if X3 sags, the rightwing may have an immediate shot. It must be noted that we use these options rarely. We have also had situations where the rightwing has been able to beat X3 and drive between X5 and X3 for an easy basket.

Another option is depicted in Diagram 3-12. After the leftwing has received a pass from the rightwing, only to be quickly covered by X4, the leftpost will often be left open. Diagram 3-13 shows further options as the wingman-cut-back pattern is carried out to the baseline series. Sometimes the zone will not adjust quickly enough, and any of the options mentioned in the baseline series becomes available. Again, the reader should review Chapter 2 for the breakdown of the baseline-series options. This will help clarify the baseline sequence in succeeding play patterns in this section.

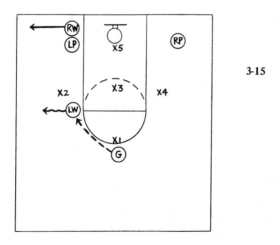

3-15

Diagram 3-14 shows an example of the give-and-go screen versus a 2-1-2 zone. The same options as in Diagrams 3-11 to 3-13 are prevalent. For example, in Diagram 3-14, if the rightpost cannot pass back to the rightwing, the leftpost picks his spot coming off the screen set by the rightwing on the weak side. If an option does

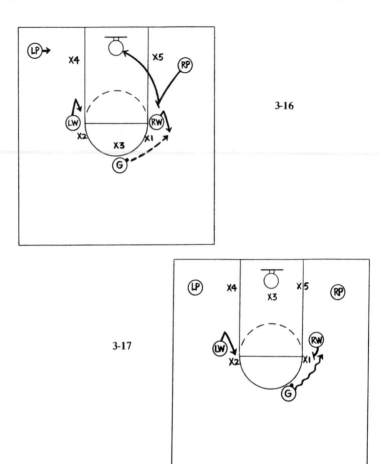

3-16

3-17

not appear, the ball is reversed to the weakside to initiate the baseline series.

Diagram 3-15 depicts our baseline-series option versus a 1-3-1 zone defense. The option that has worked most often for us is the one in which the wingman, in this case the rightwing, breaks to the corner and X5 is screened off by the leftpost. In most 1-3-1 slides the X5 man covers the corner. Frequently, the rightwing will have an unmolested shot or, if X5 fights through the block, the rightwing drops a baseline pass into the leftpost who has a layup or a close turn-around shot. If the zone is overplaying the weak-side corner, a quick pass from the leftwing to the leftpost usually results in a quick basket.

Diagram 3-16 shows our postman-roll pattern against a 3-2 zone. As depicted, one of the favorite options is when the rightwing drives off the block by the rightpost. Sometimes the rightwing has a wide-open jumper or else he has a clear lane for a layup if X4 has come too high and X5 is slow coming over. Frequently, the rightpost will be left open on the roll and the rightwing hits him with a pass for a easy basket. As an option, if

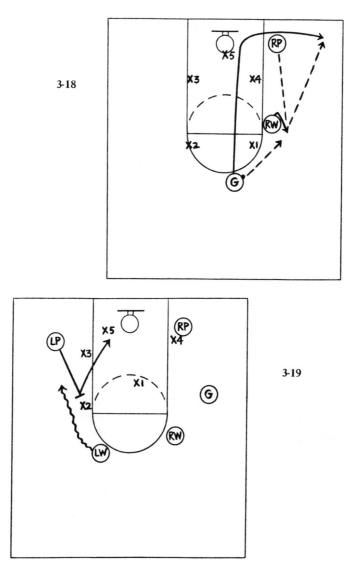

3-18

3-19

the defensive man X5 moves over to pick up the rightpost on the roll the rightpost simply drops a short pass to the leftpost who is breaking for the basket. The same options as in Diagrams 3-1 and 3-2 will work equally well versus zones. Further options include the baseline series.

Diagram 3-17 illustrates our block-and-roll pattern against a 2-3 zone. The same options as in Diagrams 3-3 to 3-7 will work against zones. Often, the guard has an open shot as the rightwing screens X1 and, if X5 covers the rightpost and X3 is slow moving over, the guard has a clear lane to drive. The guard also can hit the rightwing rolling to the basket. If none of the options unfold, the ball is reversed to the weakside for the baseline series.

Diagram 3-18 depicts our lonesome-guard reverse play pattern against a 2-2-1 zone. One of our best options is illustrated in 3-18. Sometimes the guard is open on his initial cut down the lane, but most often the guard has an unmolested shot on his break to the corner off the screen by the rightpost, as X5 becomes pinned in. If X4 slides to the corner as in some 2-2-1 slides and the rightpost has turned and closed out X5, he is often open for a pass from the guard. If these options are not open, the ball is reversed to the rightwing and then to the leftwing (Diagram 3-19), and the leftpost sets a high screen on the zone high man, usually X2, and more options unfold. If there is no play, the ball is then reversed back to the right side as the baseline series evolves with the leftpost breaking to the corner behind the rightpost's block. The same options as in Diagram 3-8 to 3-10 will work equally well against zones.

More Play-Pattern Drills

POSTMAN-ROLL DRILLS (Diagram 3-20)

1. The coach passes to the wing and the post sets a wide screen. The wing exercises all the options of the postman-roll play pattern. The wing can shoot, drive or pass to the post on his roll. The post delays until he is sure the wing has no option. The players return to their individual lines.

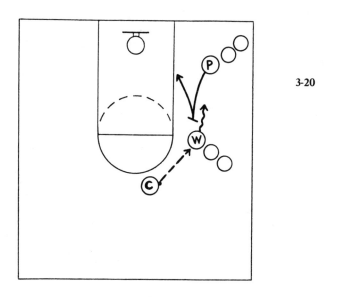

3-20

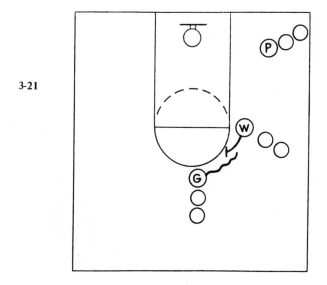

3-21

2. Add a token defense.
3. The defense goes live.
4. Run the postman roll play pattern five-on-five versus the various defenses: first a token defense, then a live defense.

BLOCK-AND-ROLL DRILLS (Diagram 3-21)

1. The wing sets a wide screen on the guard's defensive man. The guard drives, shoots or passes to the wing on a roll to the basket.
2. Add a token defense.
3. The defense goes live. The defense sagging on the postman option is added.
4. Run the block-and-roll play pattern five-on-five versus various defenses. The jumpswitch option is added. First a token defense and then a live defense is used.

LONESOME-GUARD REVERSE DRILLS (Diagram 3-22)

1. The guard passes to the wing and then fakes and breaks down the lane looking for a return pass. If he does not get pass he goes off a screen by the post. The wing exercises all of his available options.
2. Add a token defense.
3. The defense goes live.
4. Run the lonesome-guard reverse play pattern five-on-five versus the various defenses. Add the weak-side reverse option of the play pattern. First use a token defense, then a live defense.

3-22

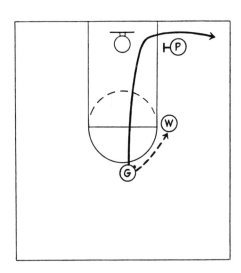

4.

Using the
Ball-Control Wishbone

A few seasons ago, I stepped into our locker room unnoticed and our leading rebounder, who stood a shade under 5'11", was staring into a large mirror and muttering to himself:

Mirror, mirror, on the wall
Who's the tallest player of all?
With most of their guys over 6'7"
Why must I be only 5'11"

Coach, perhaps your situation is not as bad or as frustrating as the one in this poem; but in high-school basketball, where teams seldom have that "big man" who can completely dominate the game, a smart, deliberate offensive strategy is crucial to success.

Although everyone appreciates the fast action associated with basketball, there is a time when it is to the smart team's advantage to slow the game to a walk. There is also a time when it is beneficial to keep ball possession until the game is over. Our teams have gained a reputation over the past few years as deliberate, ball-controlling, defense-minded basketball squads; but when we are able to, we can "go" with the ball also.

With the way things are going in today's high-scoring, fast-moving games, a team scoring 200 or more points in a game is probably not in the too-distant future. For example, during a recent season, the Indiana Pacers set a professional team-scoring record when they beat the Pittsburgh Pipers 177 to 135.

It's Time for the Slowdown

Although there is much controversy in basketball over stalling or deep-freeze tactics, I feel that there is a definite place in the game for a slowdown. In the closing moments of a game, even the die-hard enthusiast of the "run-run-run" game would find it advantageous to maintain possession. We will use the slowdown any time we feel it is necessary; but 99% of the time we slow down to *score* and not just to hold the ball. We run when we can, walk when we have to, crawl when we must. In my 10 years of coaching high-school basketball, the most points one of our teams ever scored in a single game was 116; the lowest total was 32, in a game in which the opposition scored only 19 points!

A big factor in employing the slowdown is in its psychological advantage. Success gained through the use of the slowdown in an important game is a big boost in obtaining future success. Of course, these successes can only come about through proper organization and preparation. Physical factors are almost as important as psychological ones: It is easier to run a stall if you have players with average or above-average skills in passing, dribbling and shooting.

You Must Offer Scoring Opportunities

Use a method that offers scoring opportunities. A system that does not even threaten to score will not last long. Scoring opportunities will keep the defense honest and allow the offensive team to take advantage of the defensive squad's gambling mistakes. The slowdown team should not have to gamble. They are winning and should remember that much practice in pressure situations will prepare the player and give him a feeling of confidence. If the losing team discovers that the opposition does not want to score, it will feel at liberty to gamble for the ball.

Confidence is the determining factor. The slowdown offense must be simple, taught in stages and executed with the purpose of selling it to your squad. Your players must know the "why" of the slowdown. You must explain it in detail using the same methods employed in the section at the end of Chapter 2. Let your players know why you are going to install the slowdown as a part of your game. With a few minor adjustments, you can go from the Wishbone Offense into the ball-control play patterns.

Unless the 24-second or 30-second rule is put into high-school basketball, the slowdown game will always be a favorite strategy in prep circles. The slowdown is an integral part of basketball strategy, and I am a firm opponent of its abolishment by the addition of a 24- or 30-second rule.

Teams that use the slowdown will get an unusually high number of chances at the foul stripe. This is because they will handle the ball more and probably draw more fouls from the defense. As an example of this, in a conference playoff game versus Carmel of Mundelein, we shot a conference record of 61 free throws and cashed in on 44 of them, again a conference record. The slowdown Wishbone and free-throw shooting complement themselves, as you can see.

13 Rules for the Slowdown Wishbone

1. Stay out of all danger areas; stay at least 3 ft. from all boundry lines. Corners are doubly dangerous. Avoid the 3-second lane at all costs.
2. Don't offer double-team opportunities; don't cross on offense if one of the two has the ball. You may cross if neither of the two has the ball.
3. Never allow a cross-court pass.
4. Make sure every receiver comes to meet the pass. Passers should not pass to teammates who do not come to meet the pass.
5. Use little or no dribbling. Save your dribble until you need it to get out of trouble or to drive.
6. Take only "sure" shots.
7. Try to take advantage of your best ball handlers.
8. Maintain offensive balance to spread the defense. Keep the middle open.

9. Pass sharply; do not lob.
10. Think always of scoring.
11. Don't turn your back to the goal and get double-teamed. Don't try to force a dribble between two defenders.
12. Don't gamble; the pressure is on the defense.
13. Practice to develop good free-throw shooting.

Our Success with the Banana Series

The banana and isolation patterns have been good to us. The banana will be explained in detail in this section. (See Photo 4-1.)

Photo 4-1

Actually, there are four set options to our banana pattern. They are the banana proper, the cherry, the grape and the orange. A group of players at Chesterton High School nicknamed the series the "fruit-basket" offense. By making a few simple adjustments, you can switch from the basic Wishbone to the banana series. In the initial lineup, the post players remain in their basic positions half-way to the corners. The two wings move out to approximately the parallel of the hash marks, or about 28 feet from the endline. The guard moves back approximately 30 to 35 feet from the endline (see Diagram 1-2). You are now ready to begin the banana-proper option.

When I was coaching at Chesterton, we met tourney favorite, East Chicago Roosevelt, in the semifinals of the Valparaiso Holiday JV Tournament. Our game plan was to get a lead and then go right into the banana series. We hoped to go into the "banana" early to counter Roosevelt's tremendous height and speed advantage. We grabbed a 9 to 7 lead in the first quarter and immediately went into the banana series. We stayed with the banana the remainder of the game and gradually pulled away to a 12-point upset. We later captured the first Valparaiso Tournament Championship in our school's history by beating the host club by two points.

As shown in Diagram 4-1, the guard passes to the rightwing, who has faked and come back to meet the ball. The leftwing fakes (he can also use a jab step) and cuts through with his left hand up, looking for a pass. The guard may pass to either side to start the pattern. The leftwing can go at three-quarter or full speed, depending on the situation. If he feels he can beat his defensive man, he goes full speed. If the rightwing cannot hit the leftwing, he saves his dribble in case he has no pass or is being strongly overplayed by his defensive man. The leftwing rotates with the leftpost.

In Diagram 4-2, the rightwing passes back to the guard, who has faked down occupying his defensive man. The guard has three options: If he is being overplayed, he can drive down the lane; he can pass back to the rightwing; or he can pass to the leftpost (as shown in Diagram 4-2). The only time the players from the sides (the players near the hash marks) cut through is when the ball moves from the guard to the side. The side men do not move when

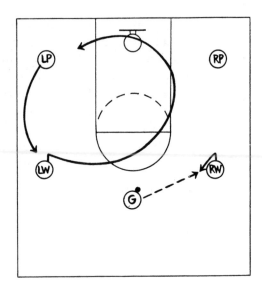

4-1

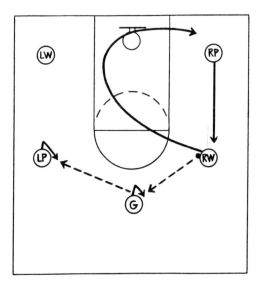

4-2

the ball is passed from the side to the guard unless they have a positive break for the basket, such as if the defensive man drops off entirely or turns his head toward the ball. In Diagram 4-2, the rightwing cuts through holding his right arm in the air looking for a pass from the leftpost.

It is also a good idea to keep the ball out of the corners, to avoid double-teaming, and to allow no cross-court passes. The entire pattern can be run like this with the ball moving from side to side. If the defense is passive, just keep moving the ball. If at any time the defensive man turns his head to watch the ball, the offensive player is instructed to go full speed for the basket.

If you have the lead and good ball handlers, this pattern will usually force the defense to play man-to-man, which is exactly what you want the opposition to do. Zone-pressure defenses are easy to beat with this pattern, or you can play "keep-away," looking for an open man near the basket. This is the opposite of what the trailing team wants you to do; so 99% of the time, they will be forced into man-to-man coverage. If the defense sags back, keep the ball moving; the responsibility and the pressure is on the defense. If the defense is behind, they will more than likely be out after the ball very soon.

In Diagram 4-3, you can see the option if the side man passes to the opposite side man. In this diagram, as the guard passes to the rightpost, the leftpost fakes and cuts through, raising his left arm and looking for the pass. After receiving the pass, the leftpost's first option is to drive all the way for the layup. If a defensive man or men drop off to clog up the lane, the leftpost will still have three other options.

As our rule states, whenever you make a pass to a player cutting down the lane, you follow it. If the player following his pass does not get a return pass from the receiver, he quickly returns to his original starting position. So another scoring option for the leftpost would be to pivot back quickly and hand off to the rightpost (Diagram 4-4), who drives hard for the basket. If the rightpost is stopped, he may pass back quickly to the leftpost, who is in good scoring position, or he may pivot back quickly and pass the ball back outside to reset the banana series. As the leftpost's third option, if he cannot pass to the rightpost or either of the side men (Diagram 4-5), he quickly pivots back and passes the ball back outside to reset. If the leftpost has none of these options, he is forced to dribble the ball back outside to reset.

Both audible and visual signals, as in the Wishbone offense, can be used in the "fruit-basket" offense. The player designated to call the play can hold up a signal, usually by a hand or finger sign, or yell out a verbal call such as "grape," "cherry," etc.

4-3

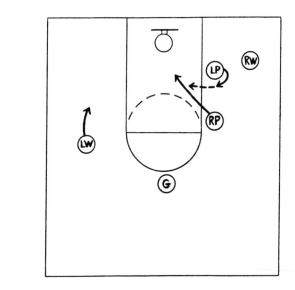

4-4

As shown in Diagram 4-6, anytime the offensive man feels he can beat his defensive man, he drives hard for the basket. In Diagram 4-6, the guard's first option is to drive all the way for the layup. If the guard is going to be stopped, he exercises the same options as the leftpost in Diagram 4-5. If a defensive man guarding

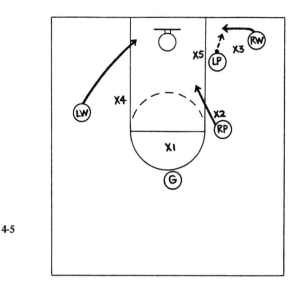

4-5

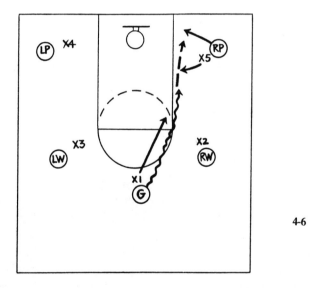

4-6

a corner man sags off, he passes to the rightpost, who breaks behind his defensive man for the layup. If the guard cannot drive all the way or pass to the open man, he quickly back pivots and passes the ball outside to reset. As a last resort, the guard can dribble back out to reset the banana series.

Our banana series also helped to win a very important game in the DeKalb Holiday Tournament against Maine East of Park Ridge. This was an especially important game for us because it was against the largest school in enrollment (4200) in Shabbona basketball history. At halftime, we led by a very slim margin but had two of our key players in foul trouble, so we decided to throw them off balance if possible with the "banana." Maine East's frontline averaged 6'5" and our frontliners were 6'3", 6'1", and 5'9". We made a slight adjustment on the usual pattern by bringing our 6'3" "big man," a very good ball handler, out to the midcourt line at the usual guard position. This, as we had hoped, brought his 6'7" defensive man with him. We also put our top scorer, our regular guard, into the big man's leftpost position. He was a good corner shooter, so we hoped to take advantage of him there. We had only eight field-goal attempts the entire second half, and we made five! We also made 18 of 19 free-throw attempts to win 60 to 49. Maine East used man-to-man, zone half-court, and full-court pressure trying to avert the banana, all to no avail.

Other Banana-Series Options— The Grape, Cherry, and Orange

CHERRY

As in any other of the play patterns, all players must fake and meet the ball from the passer. The cherry option off the banana series is shown in Diagram 4-7. The ball may be passed to either sideman to start the pattern. In Diagram 4-7, the guard passes to the rightwing and sets a fake screen on the leftwing. As soon as the guard sets the screen, he hesitates and then rolls quickly, facing the ball for the basket. He rolls with his left hand up, looking for the pass from the rightwing. If he does not receive the pass, he rotates positions with the leftpost. The leftwing exchanges positions with the guard. The leftpost goes to the leftwing's spot.

This pattern continues side to side as in Diagram 4-8. An automatic "rule" is that any time an offensive man feels he can beat his defensive adversary, he goes. Of course, this must be

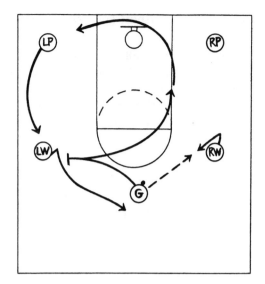

4-7

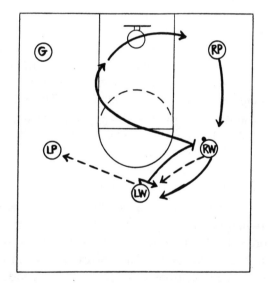

4-8

timed so as not to destroy an original play option. In Diagram 4-8, the rightwing passes back to the leftwing. The leftwing passes to the leftpost and sets a fake screen on the rightwing's defensive man. The leftwing rolls, facing the ball, and holds up his right arm looking for the pass. If the leftwing does not receive the ball, he goes to the rightpost position. The rightpost goes to the rightwing and the rightwing replaces the leftwing.

Another automatic that we follow on all banana-series patterns is that if a pass is made to the cutter, the passer immediately follows his pass. As in Diagram 4-9, the leftpost passes to the rightwing who in turn passes to the rightpost. The rightwing sets a fake screen on the leftpost and rolls, facing the ball, for a pass from the rightpost.

The first option for the rightwing is to drive all the way. If he is stopped, he exercises the same options as in Diagrams 4-4 and 4-5. He may pass to the open man, back pivot and quickly handoff to the passer (the rightpost in Diagram 4-9). He may pivot and pass the ball back outside or, as the very last resort, dribble back outside to reset. The rightpost, if he receives the ball on a back-pivot pass from the rightwing, has the same options as in Diagrams 4-4 and 4-5. Also, at any time the side men feel they can beat their defensive men in a drive for the basket, they exercise all the options as in Diagram 4-6.

As an alternate option for the cherry pattern:

If after a few times the defense adjusts or overplays to the fake screen on the side man, you counter with the pattern shown in Diagram 4-10. The guard passes to the rightwing and then sets a permanent screen on the leftwing. The leftwing hesitates, then fakes and cuts hard off the screen, looking for a pass from the rightwing. The leftwing can cut either inside or outside the screen. The guard rolls back to the top of the key area after the leftwing goes off his screen. The leftpost rotates to the leftwing position. The leftwing goes to the leftpost's spot.

As shown in Diagram 4-11, after the rightwing passes to the leftwing he automatically follows his pass. The leftwing now exercises all the options as in Diagrams 4-4 and 4-5. If the rightwing receives the back-pivot pass from the leftwing, he also has the same options as in Diagrams 4-4 and 4-5. Also in Diagram 4-11, the side man (rightwing) can drive and exercise all the options as in Diagram 4-6.

Another example of our banana series in action occured a few years ago when we played Kirkland Hiawatha High School.

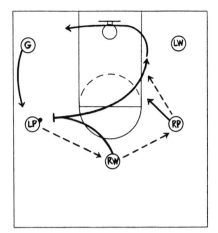

4-9

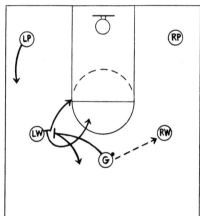

4-10

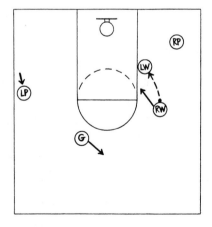

4-11

Kirkland was a high-scoring team and was unbeaten, having won their first three games by over 30-point margins. We held a team meeting and decided to slow Kirkland down with our "banana" to see if we could throw their run-and-shoot game off.

We jumped off to an early 20 to 4 lead as our opponents continually turned the ball over in an effort to speed up the game. This early spurt was to be the difference in the game as we hung on for a 54 to 48 victory. Our opponents took 43 shots and made 19 while we made only 27 field-goal attempts and canned 18, for 67%! We were outrebounded by 16 caroms and Kirkland made 16 more field-goal attempts, but we won by six points!

GRAPE

Again, the play may be run to either side of the floor. In Diagram 4-12, the guard passes to the rightwing. At the same time, the leftwing sets a screen on the rightpost's defensive man. The leftpost takes the leftwing's position out front at the side. The rightpost fakes toward the endline then comes back out trying to rub off his defensive man on the leftwing's screen. After the rightpost has come over the top, the leftwing rolls facing the ball to a low-post spot, looking for the ball. If the rightpost does not receive the ball, he circles to his original position. If the leftwing does not get the ball, he takes the leftpost's position.

In Diagram 4-13, the rightwing passes to the guard and the guard hits the leftpost. The pass can be returned immediately to the original passer, for example: the rightwing passes to the guard, the guard passes back to the rightwing and the pattern begins on the same side of the floor. In Diagram 4-13, the rightwing sets a screen on the leftwing's defensive man. The rightpost comes out to the right side position. The leftwing fakes toward the endline then comes back out trying to rub off his defensive man on rightwing's screen. After the leftwing has come over the top, the rightwing rolls, facing the ball, to a low-post position looking for the ball. If the leftwing does not get the ball, he returns to his original position. The rightwing takes the rightpost slot.

In Diagram 4-14, the pass has gone from the rightpost to the rightwing coming off the screen by the leftpost. The rightwing has

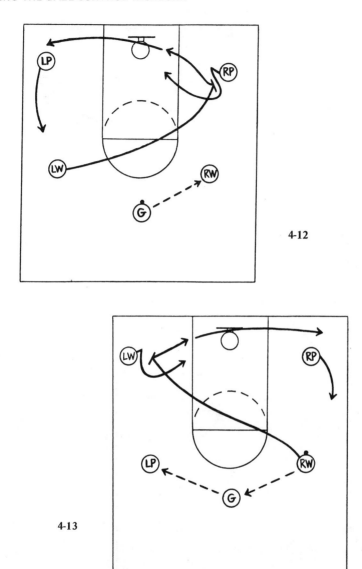

4-12

4-13

four options: First, he may shoot or drive all the way for a layup. If the rightwing is stopped by a defensive maneuver, he may pass to the leftpost, who is rolling to the basket, as in Diagram 4-15. He may also pass to the rightpost who is carrying out the automatic rule of following your pass. As another possibility, the rightwing could pass to the leftwing who breaks behind his defensive man.

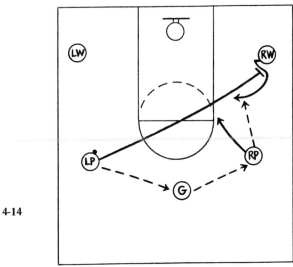

4-14

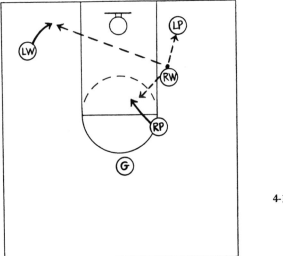

4-15

If the rightwing has none of the options, he pivots back quickly to get the ball outside or else he dribbles the ball out if necessary to reset to another pattern. Diagram 4-16 shows an automatic option for the cornerman on the screen from the sideline. If the defensive man is overplaying strongly to come out over the top of the screen, the rightpost (in Diagram 4-16) fakes to come high and then bursts low for the basket and receives a high pass from the sideman.

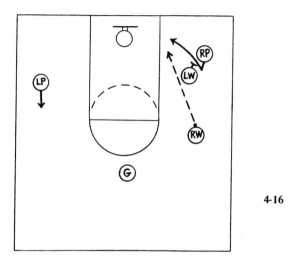

4-16

ORANGE

In the orange option, the guard passes either right or left to start the pattern. In Diagram 4-17, the guard passes to the rightwing. Simultaneously, the rightpost comes up and sets a screen on the rightwing's defensive man. The rightwing fakes a drive left and then drives hard right. If the way is clear, he can drive all the way for the layup. If not, he can pass to the rightpost who delays and then rolls for the basket facing the ball. If there is no play the guard stops and quickly pivots back to return the pass to the guard. The guard starts another pattern. The rightpost returns to his original position.

As an alternate move: If after a few attempts at the orange option the rightwing (as in Diagram 4-18) is strongly overplayed to the right, he fakes a drive right and goes left. If the way is clear, he drives all the way. Another option is the short-range jumper. If stopped by a sagging defender, he can pass to the defender's man, who breaks to the basket. The players all return to their original positions.

We use the orange option as an automatic versus a man-to-man pressure situation when the passer has no outlet to pass. The cornermen are instructed to automatically come up and set a screen in this situation.

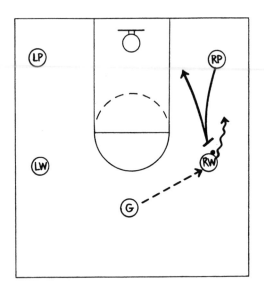

4-17

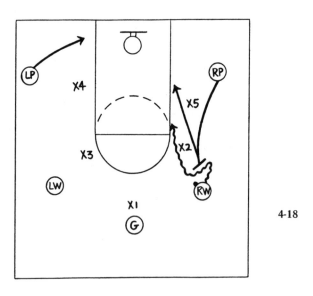

4-18

Banana-Series Drills

The following are our favorite ball-control banana-series drills. These drills have been tried and have proved quite effective for us.

1. THREE-MISTAKE DRILL

We run our first team against our second unit with both squads using all of the banana-series options. One team will continue on offense until they commit "three mistakes." A mistake is a turnover of any kind, a missed shot rebounded by the defense, or an offensive foul. When the offense scores, it is one point for a basket and one point for each free throw. Regardless of who rebounds a missed free throw, the ball goes back to the offensive team. When the offense commits its third mistake, the ball goes over to the defense. The defensive team now becomes the offensive team for "three mistakes." A running score is kept. We have also run our regular Wishbone-Offense play patterns in this drill.

2. ONE-MISTAKE DRILL

We set the scoreboard clock at three minutes. One team has the ball until it commits "one mistake." A mistake is defined in drill number one. When a mistake is committed, the ball goes over to the defensive team. The same scoring is used as in drill number one. This drill simulates actual game conditions as you are racing the clock. All free throws are of the one-and-one type.

3. SEVEN-ON-FIVE OR EIGHT-ON-FIVE

We run seven defensive men against our five offensive men. Then we run eight defensive men against our five. We have found this drill to have given our players great confidence in their ball-handling ability as they find it much easier to beat five-on-five than seven- or eight-on-five. I have been fortunate to have had teams that have been able to keep the ball for eight to ten minutes without a turnover. This drill has proved to be a great help in late game situations.

4. MOST TIME ON THE CLOCK

We run this drill rarely because it conflicts with our philosophy of always trying to score while in our ball-control offense. One team runs the banana series trying only to hold the ball, not trying to score. When the offensive team loses the ball, the total time consumed is noted. The defense then goes to offense and attempts to hold the ball for a longer time period than the first team. This is an excellent drill for rare occasions in a season when you want to go into a "deep-freeze" offense.

5. TWO-VERSUS-THREE LEADUP DRILL

As a leadup drill to the previous four drills, we have two offensive men handle the ball against three defensive players. The first offensive man dribbles to free himself from pressure by two of the defensive men. He learns to control the ball and be relaxed under pressure. The second offensive man, by fakes and cuts, attempts to free himself for a pass. Rotate all five players to give everyone an opportunity in each situation.

5.

Perfecting Variations on Basketball's Wishbone Offense

Many variations can be run off the regular Wishbone-Offense player-placement patterns. In this chapter, we will illustrate in detail three of the variations that have been quite successful for us: the *Green*, the *Isolation pattern*, and the *Gold*. All of these patterns, as in the banana series, work quite effectively after you have forced the defense into man-for-man coverage.

The Green pattern helped us win a pivotal game en route to the West Suburban Catholic Championship during a recent season. Aurora Marmion had beaten us by one point on our court in early December. Since that defeat, we reeled off 11 consecutive wins and were now facing Aurora on their home court in what was described as the big "showdown" game.

We had not used the Green pattern in four years, but on Tuesday we installed the offense in preparation for Friday's big game, hoping to surprise Aurora. We won the game 73 to 39 by making 20 of 31 field-goal attempts and 33 of 39 free-throw attempts, as Aurora fouled excessively in the second half. We had an amazing total of 39 free-throws attempted compared to only 31 field-goal attempts. We were 85% from the foul line and 65% from the field for the game. Our starting five scored 16, 15, 14, 10 and 8 points. You can see the balance of the offensive pattern.

The Green Pattern

As depicted in Diagram 5-1, the lonesome guard initiates the offense approximately 23 feet from the basket. The wings are wide, similar to the banana series, approximately 22 feet from the basket. The posts start in a tight formation with one foot near the first black circle near the lane. As in all Wishbone patterns, the offense can be run to either side of the floor. This pattern has good continuity as you simply move the ball from side to side until a good shot becomes available.

In Diagram 5-1, the rightwing fakes low and then comes back to meet the pass from the guard. It should be noted here that any time an offensive player is being overplayed, he should fake and cut immediately to the basket.

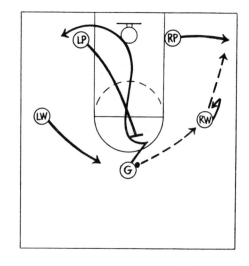

5-1

As the rightwing receives the guard's pass, the leftpost comes to the high-post area to set a pick on the guard's defensive man. The leftpost sets a wide screen but makes sure he does not draw an offensive foul for being too close on the blind side of the guard's defensive man. At the same time the leftpost is moving up to the high-post area to set his screen, the rightpost breaks for the corner to receive a pass from the rightwing.

The rightpost receives the ball while on the move and immediately pivots, facing his defensive man. The lonesome guard has rubbed off his defensive man by faking right and coming back left, rubbing his man on the leftpost's screen. Sometimes the guard will be left wide open, but if he is not open, he breaks sharply to the left and comes back out high in the leftwing's offensive area. The leftwing has already replaced the guard at the top of the key for defensive and outlet purposes.

If the rightpost cannot pass into the lonesome guard and cannot fake and take his man one-on-one on the baseline, he looks for the leftpost, who rolls down the lane (Diagram 5-2). If the rightpost cannot hit the leftpost he passes back to the rightwing and the leftpost breaks sharply to the weak-side low-post area. As illustrated in Diagram 5-2, the rightwing then passes back to the leftwing who meets the pass. The leftwing then passes to the lonesome guard, who fakes low and comes back to meet the pass as the same pattern is now started on the left side of the floor.

As shown in Diagram 5-2, as the leftwing passes to the guard, the rightpost sets a wide screen in the high-post area on the leftwing's defensive man. In diagram 5-3, as the leftpost breaks to the left corner and receives a pass from the guard, he turns and faces his defensive man. The leftwing has faked left and gone back right, rubbing off his defensive man on the rightpost's screen. If the leftwing does not receive a pass from the leftpost, he breaks to the right sharply and comes back out high in the rightwing's area. The rightwing replaces the leftwing.

If the leftpost cannot pass to the leftwing or if he cannot take his defensive man one-on-one, he looks for the rightpost (Diagram 5-4), who rolls down the lane. If the leftpost cannot pass to the rightpost, he back passes to the guard and the rightpost breaks sharply to the weak-side low-post area. The guard then passes to the rightwing and the entire pattern is ready to begin on the right side.

Diagram 5-5 depicts an automatic situation when the defense is overplaying. For example, in Diagram 5-5, as X5 is overplaying the rightpost, the rightpost gives a quick fake and jab step and breaks for the basket for an easy shot. The offensive man should at all times look for this situation.

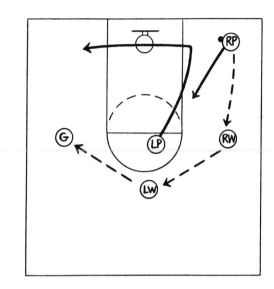

5-2

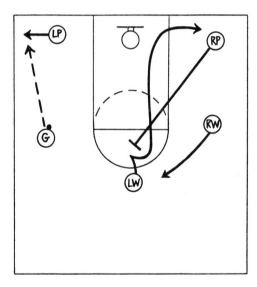

5-3

The key rules to remember are:
1. Always meet the pass to protect the ball.
2. If overplayed, break to the basket.
3. Be patient and wait for the scoring opportunity to develop. This is also an excellent pattern to use late in a game in which you are leading, as it usually forces the defense into mistakes.

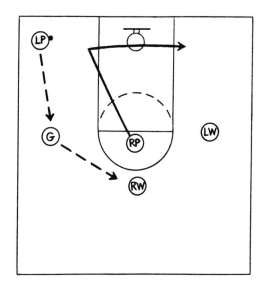

5-4

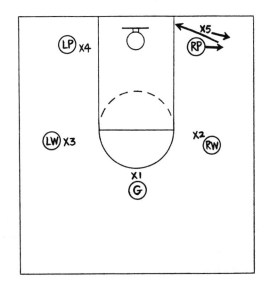

5-5

Isolation Pattern

The isolation pattern has worked quite well for us and is used only on "spot" occasions during the season. On rare occasions, we have used the offense for an entire game.

The isolation gives you the advantage of using your best

one-on-one player in a crucial situation; this usually affords him the largest percentage of scoring opportunities. It can also give you the opportunity of setting up a weak defender by putting his offensive man in the "isolation" slot.

This pattern, just as the green pattern, is quite effective when you have forced the defense into a man-coverage situation. If you have a lead, the offense becomes very tenacious as it forces the defense to come out after the ball. If the defense sags, you just move the ball until the defense comes out after you.

An example of a rare occasion in which we used the isolation for a complete game is the Waterman contest a few seasons ago. Waterman was the early favorite for the conference title and featured a veteran front line averaging 6'5". We used our best one-on-one player, 5'9" Rod Fultz, in the isolation slot. Fultz hit on 10 of 15 field-goal attempts and 14 of 18 free throws for 34 of our winning 53 points. (The final score was 53 to 50.) As a team we made 15 of 27 field-goal attempts! This was Waterman's first loss in conference play and it helped pave the way for our third consecutive conference title.

As depicted in Diagram 5-6, the number-one offensive man's starting position would be about 23-25 feet from the basket. The number-two offensive man, your best one-on-one player, play's in the isolation slot about 23 feet from the basket. If your number-two player is left-handed he should set up on the left side of the floor. The number-three position is for your poorest ball handler, usually your big man. He is your safety man; but if his defensive man turns his head, he is instructed to break to the basket. He sets up about 28 feet from the basket.

The number four- and five-positions, usually your other guard and best ball-handling forward, play in the corner in a tandem and rotate positions with the number-one man. They set up deep in the corner.

The first option, as shown in Diagram 5-6, starts as the number-two man sets a wide screen (feet spread wide, hands at side) on the number-one man's defensive player. The number-one player can drive all the way to the basket, jump-shoot or hit the number-two man, who rolls belly to the ball for the basket. The number-two man comes back to his original position if he does not get the ball on his roll to the basket. As the last two players work their options, the number-five player is breaking to the top of the key area to replace number one.

If number one finds no available option, he passes back to number five and then he breaks to the weak side, replacing number five and behind number four in a tandem. The number--three player is a defensive safety and also an outlet man if the ball handlers get in a jam.

Again, anytime a player is being overplayed, he is instructed to break to the basket. Also, if a defensive man drops off to double-team another player, the player (whose man has dropped off) is instructed to yell "double-team" and break for the basket. If the defense sags off or fails to put pressure on number one and number two, just pass the ball back and forth, occasionally bring in number three to force the defense to come after the ball. As another rule, the other players not involved in the pattern must keep their defensive men occupied, always looking for a quick break to the basket. Also, the players are instructed not to dribble unless they have to.

Diagram 5-7 illustrates one of our favorite options. The number-two man takes two or three short steps towards the ball and the number-one man fakes a pass to him. If the defensive man overplays number two, which he must to get the ball, number two

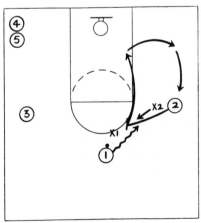

5-6

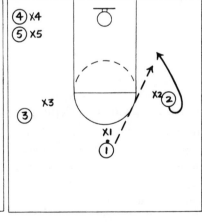

5-7

quickly pivots on his left leg and rolls to the basket looking for a pass from number one. If the defensive man sags on number two, number two simply returns a pass to number one.

Diagram 5-8 depicts another option. Number one passes to number two and then fakes left and breaks down the lane looking for a return pass. If number one does not get a return pass, he breaks to the weak side, replacing number five behind number four in a corner tandem. Number five has broken to the top of the key area on number one's pass to number two. Number two may also take his man one-on-one on this option. If number two has no option, he passes back to number five to reset another option.

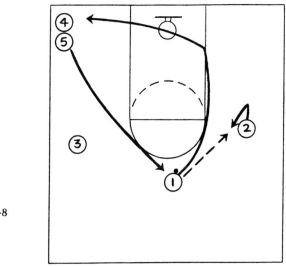

5-8

Diagram 5-9 shows still another option as number one passes to number two and then sets a screen on number three's defensive man. Number three fakes left and then rubs off his man on the screen. If number three does not receive a pass, he returns to his original position as does number one. Number two also has the one-on-one option here.

Diagram 5-10 depicts another option. As in Diagram 5-8, when number one passes to number two, he then breaks down the lane and replaces number five. Number five bursts out hard as if coming to the top of the key. He stops suddenly and loops for the basket, looking for a pass from number two for a short hook or turnaround.

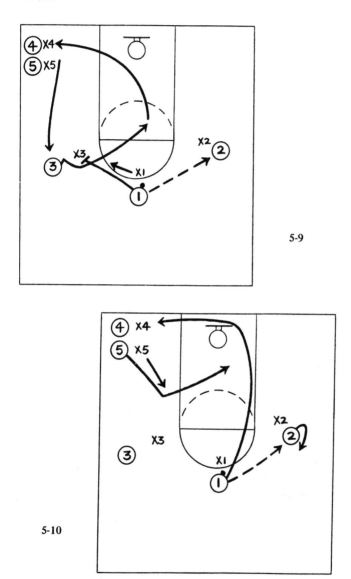

5-9

5-10

Diagrams 5-11 and 5-12 are examples of the defense "going to sleep" on our offensive men. In 5-11, on number one's pass to number two, number four's defensive man has turned his head or is not watching him closely. Number four immediately breaks for the basket. This surprisingly simple maneuver has scored several baskets for us. In Diagram 5-12, a similar situation, number three catches his man asleep and busts hard for the basket.

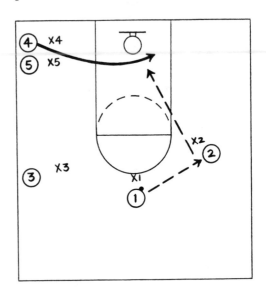

5-11

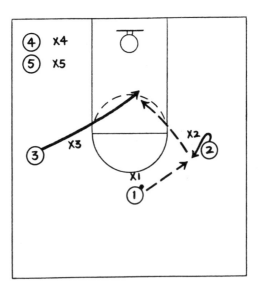

5-12

Various options appear, such as in Diagram 5-12, if X5 would come up to cover number three then number three could drop off a short pass to number five, who busts to the basket after seeing X5 make his move to cover number three.

Several times, we have tried to take advantage of a poor defender by putting his man in the isolation slot. For instance, we can put our center in the isolation slot when we know that his man is a poor defender. Teams have countered this move by putting their best defensive man on whomever we have in the isolation slot. Recently, during one important tournament game, our opponents switched defensive men putting, their 5'9" guard (their best defensive man) on our 6'4" center, who was playing the isolation slot. We countered this move as shown in Diagram 5-13. We simply had our center (number five) roll to the basket to set up a mismatch situation on the 5'9" defender.

Diagram 5-14 depicts a situation in which a double-team forms when X4 and X1 double-team ball handler number one. Number four immediately yells "double-team" to number one and breaks to the basket.

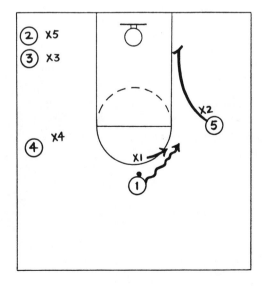

5-13

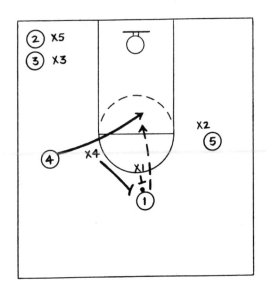

5-14

SUMMARY OF ISOLATION RULES

1. If you have a left-hander in the isolation spot (the one-on-one position), originate on the left side of the floor.
2. Anytime an offensive player is being overplayed, he should fake and then bust for the basket.
3. Take your time; the pressure is on the defense. The score and the clock are in your favor.
4. Be careful on your cuts not to clog up the strong side of the floor.
5. Do not dribble until it is absolutely necessary to do so.
6. Meet all passes and protect the ball.
7. Keep the ball moving unless the defense is sagging.
8. All players must keep their defensive men occupied.
9. When an offensive player sees his defensive man going toward a double-team he must warn his teammates and then break to the basket.

The Gold Pattern

We also use the gold pattern on spot occasions. This is a pattern with continuous movement. First a block-and-roll is performed by the postman and wingman, then a screen by the postman on the opposite postman, and finally a backdoor play with the guard passing to the post and the wingman cutting for the basket.

The player alignment is the same as in the green pattern depicted in Diagrams 5-1 through 5-5. The lonesome guard initiates the action approximately 23 feet from the basket. The posts start in a tight formation with one foot near the first black circle near the lane. (The gold pattern can be run to either side of the floor.) As in the green pattern, there is good continuity as you simply move the ball from side to side until a percentage shot develops.

In Diagram 5-15, the guard passes to the rightwing and, simultaneously, the rightpost sets a screen on the rightwing's defensive man. The guard can drive, shoot or pass to the rightpost who delays for a second and then rolls quickly to the basket. If these three options are unavailable, the rightwing picks up the ball and passes back to the guard who has sprinted towards the ball.

As illustrated in 5-15, the rightpost has rolled through (if he did not receive the pass) and has set a screen on the leftpost's defensive man. The leftpost fakes low and attempts to rub his man off on the rightpost's screen. As an alternative, the leftpost can fake high and go low off the screen. If the leftpost does not receive a pass from the guard he continues to the strong side of the floor and takes the post position on the right side of the floor.

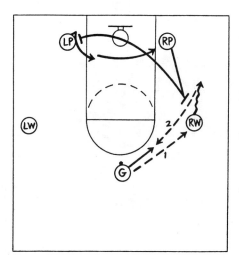

5-15

Diagram 5-16 depicts the next continuous move. The rightpost, now on the left side of the floor, breaks to the high-post area for a pass from the guard. The instant the pass is made, the leftwing goes backdoor. The leftwing hopes that his defensive man has turned his head to look at the pass from the guard to the rightpost. If this happens, an easy layup for the leftwing usually results. If the rightpost cannot pass to the leftwing on the backdoor option, he can shoot a medium-range jumper or he can fake a shot and drive for the basket.

Diagram 5-17 illustrates the rightpost's next move if he has none of the available options. The rightpost passes back to the guard and then rolls to the leftpost area. The guard then passes to the leftwing, who is moving back to his original position after going backdoor on the previous sequence.

In Diagram 5-18, the rightpost now comes high and sets a screen on the leftwing's defensive man. All of the options, as in 5-15, are now available on the left side of the floor. The rightpost, if not receiving the ball, now rolls and sets a screen on the leftpost's defensive man and any of the available options, as in 5-15, take place.

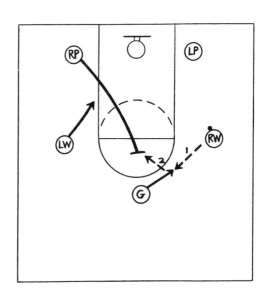

5-16

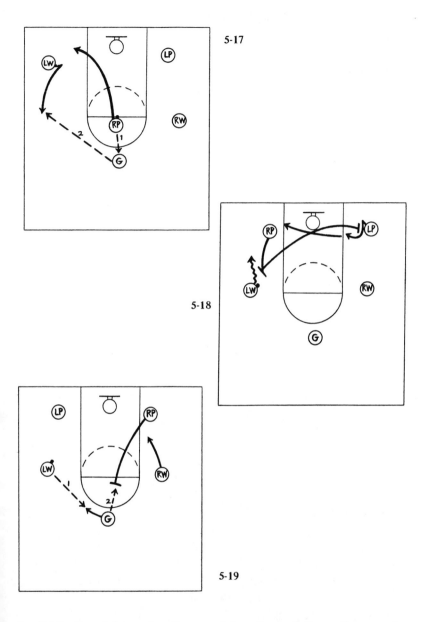

5-17

5-18

5-19

In 5-19, the rightpost, after receiving the ball from the guard, now has the backdoor option with the rightwing as depicted in 5-16

Isolation-Pattern Drills

We use the following drills when working on our Isolation pattern:

1. ONE-ON-ONE OVERPLAY DRILL

As seen in Diagram 5-20, X1, the defensive player, overplays the offensive player number one. The coach tosses the ball to number one to start action and the coach can also be used as an outlet man by number one. The offensive player tries to fake and reverse his position and go backdoor.

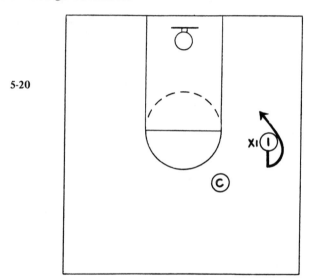

5-20

2. GUARD-WING OPTION DRILL

The guard and wingmen go through the options illustrated in Diagrams 5-21, 5-22 and 5-23.
   a. The guard and wingmen go over the options with no defense.
   b. A token or passive defense is added.
   c. The defense goes live.
   d. Add five defensive players and five offensive players and go live.

e. Rotate players to all positions.
f. Lefthanded players in the isolation slot should set up on the left side of the court.

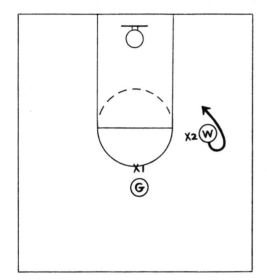

5-21

5-22

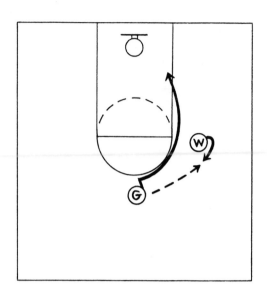

5-23

3. THREE-MISTAKE DRILL, ONE-MISTAKE DRILL AND SEVEN-ON-FIVE DRILL.

We run these drills (detailed in Chapter 4), substituting the isolation pattern for the banana-series patterns.

6.

Attacking the Presses with Basketball's Wishbone Offense

Pressure defenses become more popular each year, and no change in this trend can be foreseen in the near future. Pressure defenses have evolved from a last-minute desperation maneuver to what is now a full-game strategy for many teams. As in almost any other phase of basketball, organization is the key. A well-coached team will know through advance planning and practice exactly what to do in each situation that is likely to occur during a game. Pressure-defense teams thrive on teams that are poorly organized.

The lack of good passers and ball handlers has made the pressing defenses more effective. You simply can't hide weak passers when playing against pressure defenses; so unless your team works hard on proper ball handling, most presses will beat you. The players must understand the objectives of the press offense, how it works, and what each teammate is doing. There are ways to beat any kind of defense if you understand it and are willing to spend the time developing good practice habits.

The players must have a positive attitude. If they fear a press they will tend to panic. Practice builds confidence and well-drilled players are not apt to panic. Give your players drills, drills and more drills.

In preparation for pressure defenses it is important to simplify your attack. A team must have a pattern and a plan of attack, but a coach must provide a flexible system, with certain freelance options. Each press is different, with different strengths and weaknesses. Again, ball handling and simplicity are the keys to success. A good press can be devastating. We won a conference championship game a few years ago by scoring eight points off our pressure defense in the last 20 seconds to eke out a two-point win.

Through scouting, the coach should be ready to prepare his team for the pressure defense. He should have thorough knowledge of the strengths and weaknesses of the opponent's press, for this knowledge makes the attacking plan easier.

If a coach expects to win his share of close games each season or hopes to be a consistent winner, he should be certain that his team is prepared to meet the pressure defenses. At Elgin, we try to use a general plan of attack against all man-to-man and zone pressure defenses, although we may adjust our attack plan depending on the opposing team's defensive adjustments.

Psychologically, the coach must prepare his team not to be upset by pressure teams. Structurally, pressing defenses are the weakest defenses in basketball, because they overplay or double-team opponents. Double-teaming leaves many openings in the defensive structure, and if the ball can escape the double-team successfully, the offense automatically has a one-man advantage. Man-to-man and zone presses attempt to do in a full-court area (approximately 84 by 54 feet) what is difficult to do in an area 20 feet from the basket: prevent the opposing team from scoring points.

Why the Opponents Use Pressure Defenses

The following are the main reasons why teams use pressure defenses:

1. Pressure defenses try to wear the opposition down, mentally and physically.
2. They hope to control the tempo of a game.
3. Some teams fear pressure and lose their poise.
4. Some teams practice only half-court or scrimmage very little on a full-court basis.
5. Some coaches don't teach or use the pressure defense; therefore, they don't practice much against it.

6. Some teams are not fundamentally sound.
7. The press tends to knock a pattern team out of its offensive timing.
8. A press keeps the big man away from the basket. It helps to equalize a height disadvantage.

Attacking Full-Court Zone Pressure

Diagram 6-1 shows our press-attack formation against all types of full-court zone presses. We usually have one of our wings (the best ball handler) take the ball out. However, during early practice sessions we rotate our players at all five positions. In case of injury or for substitution purposes, our players know the other positions. It also gives our players better knowledge of the possibilities of the other positions.

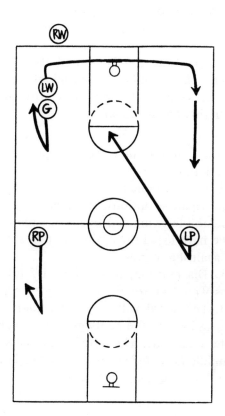

6-1

ess instructed otherwise, we have the rightwing take the ball out to the right side of the backboard (to the rightwing's right-handed side). Diagram 6-1 depicts the leftwing breaking to the weak side of the floor. The leftwing hesitates briefly near the left corner as a potential receiver. If he does not receive the pass he continues down the weak side. The rightwing actually has four potential receivers: First, he can pass to the guard, who has faked deep and then busted back towards the ball. The guard must be warned not to get pinned in too deep near the endline or sideline. Occasionally, the guard may receive a pass wide open as he has faked long near the mid-court area. Second, the rightwing can pass to the leftpost who has faked long and broken to the middle area. Third, the rightwing can pass to the leftwing on the weak side of the floor. As a fourth option, the rightwing can pass to the rightpost, who has faked and gone long down the court. The rightpost comes back upcourt only if help is needed.

Whoever is the receiver of the first pass starts the option. For example, in Diagram 6-2, if the rightwing made his initial pass to the leftpost breaking to the middle, the leftpost can pivot and drop a pass to the guard (as in 6-2) or the leftwing on the weak side. The guard can then dribble to the middle in a fast-break situation with the leftwing and the rightpost, with the leftpost as the trailer and the rightwing as the safety.

Diagrams 6-3 through 6-6 describe our press zone offense against the standard full-court presses: the 2-1-2, 1-2-1-1, 2-2-1, and 1-2-2. We have described one of the many options against each standard press. On separate options, the rightwing passes to the guard, the leftpost, the leftwing and finally the rightpost. For the sake of brevity, we have listed the options in this way. Any of the options will work against any press.

For example, in Diagram 6-3, versus the 2-1-2 full-court press, one of the options would be for the rightwing to make his initial pass to the guard. The guard will usually be trapped by X1 and X3. The guard passes back to the rightwing, who quickly passes to the leftwing on the weak side. The leftwing can pass to the guard breaking to the middle (as in 6-3) or dribble the ball quickly down the sideline. The leftwing joins the guard and rightpost in a fast-break situation with the leftpost as the trailer and the rightwing as the safetyman.

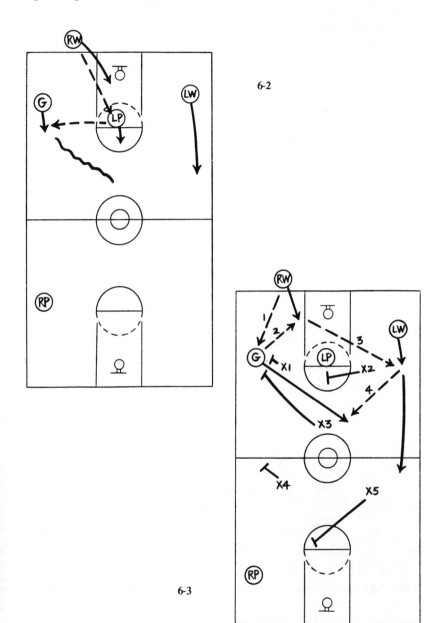

6-2

6-3

Diagram 6-4 shows another one of the various options versus the 2-2-1 press. The rightwing initiates the action with a quick pass to the leftpost, who has busted in the middle area. In most 2-2-1 presses, X3 and X4 will trap the leftpost. In 6-4, the leftpost pivots quickly and passes to the guard, who receives the pass and then breaks to the middle for a fast-break situation with the leftwing and rightpost, with the leftpost as the trailer and the rightwing as the safety.

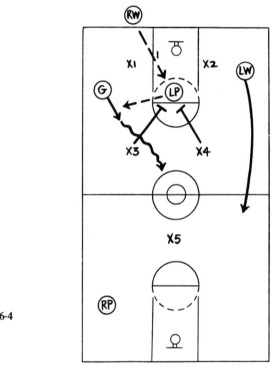

6-4

Diagram 6-5 illustrates another option versus the 1-2-1-1 press. In 6-5, the rightwing passes to the leftwing, who, in most presses, will be trapped by X4 and X3. The leftwing passes to the leftpost, who has moved toward the sideline. The leftpost should be trapped by X4 and X1. In this situation, the leftpost passes to the rightwing, who has broken to an open area in the middle. The rightwing now joins the guard and the rightpost (who has moved across court) in a fast-break situation with the leftwing the trailer, and the leftpost, the safety.

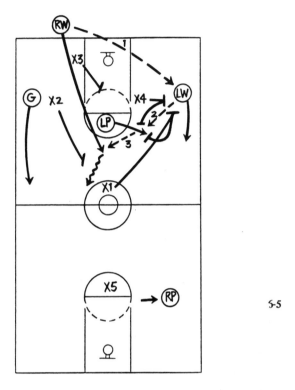

6-5

Diagram 6-6 depicts one of our options versus the 1-2-2 press. In this example, the rightwing makes a direct pass to the rightpost, who has slipped by the defense. We get this option on rare occasions, but it usually ends up in an unchallenged basket.

As previously stated, any of the options will work against any press. For example, versus the 2-2-1 press in Diagram 6-7 the rightwing can pass to the guard to initiate action. The guard can pass to the leftpost breaking to the middle (as in 6-7) or the leftwing on the extreme weak side. The guard can also pass back to the rightwing and the rightwing has two or three immediate options: He can pass directly to the leftpost (as in 6-4) or he has the possibilities of passing long to the rightpost or to the leftwing streaking down the weak side.

6-6

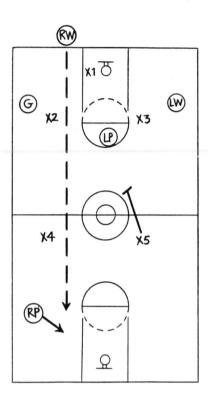

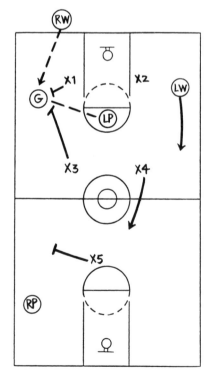

6-7

Diagram 6-8 illustrates a simple option we once used to win an important conference game. Our opponents were in a 1-2-1-1 press, with the score tied and four seconds remaining. The rightwing faked a pass to the guard, getting X2 and X1 to lean in that direction. X3 plugged the middle, fronting the leftpost. X4 had leaned toward the strong side of the floor, ready to pick up the rightpost who was breaking back upcourt to help out. The defensive mistake was made when X5 also cheated up on the strong side with the rightpost looking for a possible interception. Our leftwing sprinted down the weak side, and spotted by the rightwing, was wide open for the layup.

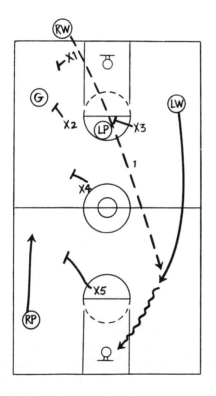

6-8

In Diagram 6-9, we show our player alignment if the ball is taken out on the right side of the court (the rightwing's left side). The action is reversed with the leftwing hesitating and then breaking down the weak side on the left side of the floor. The guard takes a few steps, fakes long and then breaks back to the middle area for help. The leftpost goes long and only comes back up the court if help is definitely needed.

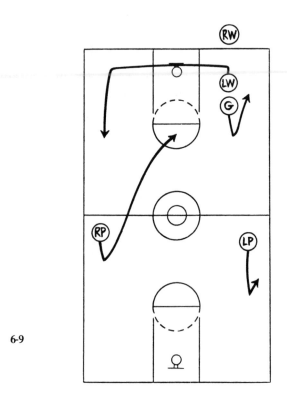

6-9

Diagram 6-10 shows our press offense against three-quarter–court zone pressure. The only adjustment we make is to move our offensive alignment deeper. In 6-10, we are facing a 1-2-1-1 three-quarter press, and the rightwing has passed to the guard in the free-throw area. The leftwing has broken down the weak side and the leftpost has broken to the middle in the mid-court area. The rightpost has also gone deeper than he usually would.

Diagram 6-11 illustrates a "change-of-pace" offense against a full zone press. We use this offense occasionally to confuse the opponents, especially when our opponents have been in a certain type of press for a long period of time. We call this our

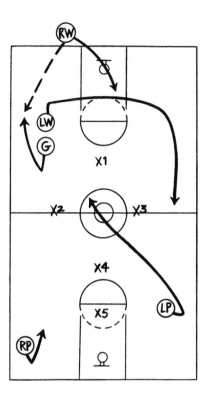

6-10

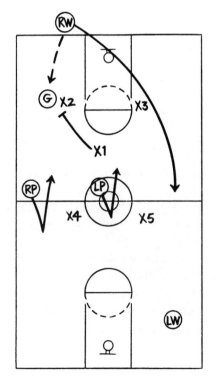

6-11

Three-Across pattern. Diagram 6-11 depicts the three-across versus a 2-1-2 press. The rightpost and leftpost line up on the ten-second line with the rightpost on the left side and the leftpost in the middle of the court. The leftwing goes long on the right side. The rightwing passes to the guard and the rightwing breaks to the weak side of the court near the ten-second area. The rightpost and leftpost both fake long for a few steps and then break back towards the ball. We have found this pattern to be very effective, especially after using a regular pattern for a quarter or two. The initial option is for the guard to pass to one of the three-across players (the rightpost, leftpost, or rightwing).

Attacking Half-Court Zone Pressure

SHABBONA SAGA

Diagrams 6-12 and 6-13 illustrate two Wishbone options against a half-court zone pressure defense. We used these two options against Shabbona High School in a recent Super-Sectional championship game at DeKalb.

Shabbona was the state tournament's last unbeaten team at 28-0. This game had extra meaning to our coaching staff because it was against a school we had previously coached, and it also meant that the winner advanced to the "Elite 8" state finals. Shabbona had built its reputation on fine shooting and a stingy half-court press, and the team was coached by my former assistant, Dave Fultz. Shabbona had held its opponents to an amazingly low 41 points per game.

We knew that to beat Shabbona we had to solve the problem of their half-court pressure. We had only three days to practice for the game because we won the sectional championship on Friday and were to meet Shabbona on Tuesday. Our scouting report stated that Shabbona would not always front our strong-side postman and that they would usually leave the weak-side post area open.

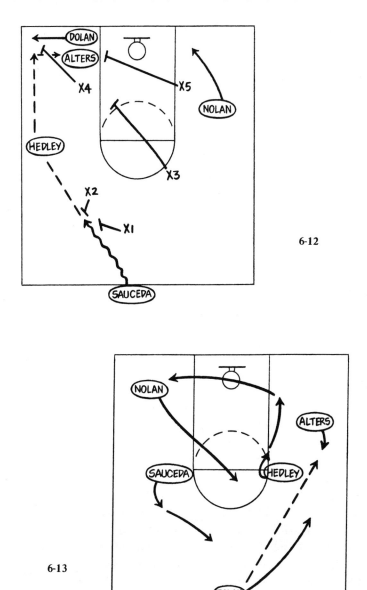

6-12

6-13

We decided to go directly into our baseline series. This gave us an automatic overload. We put our regular lonesome guard, Chris Dolan, on the baseline as the swing man. Our center, Kay Alters, was stationed in the leftpost area, closing out any man in that zone. Craig Hedley was the leftwing, Bob Sauceda was at lonesome guard and Jeff Nolan was the rightpost on the weak side. Our game plan was to force Shabbona to overplay Dolan on the second pass. As shown in Diagram 6-12, Dolan would then pass to Alters, who had closed out the man in his area. This pass would draw X5 and X3 to cover Alters. Alters would quickly pass to Nolan who was breaking hard from the weak side. This worked several times. Alters also had options to shoot or drive.

In the later stages of the second quarter, Shabbona made defensive adjustments, and we countered with another slight change. We simply broke Sauceda (Diagram 6-13) from his leftwing position out high and moved Hedley to a high-post position. On the pass from the lonesome guard Dolan to rightpost Alters, Hedley would roll down immediately, looking for a pass. If Hedley did not receive a pass, he would then go to the weak side, replacing Nolan, who was breaking to the high-post area. Nolan would then roll, looking for a pass. This simple pattern garnered three key baskets in the fourth quarter and also netted our winning basket by Nolan at the buzzer in overtime, pulling out a 56-54 victory in a classic game.

Diagram 6-14 depicts one of our patterns against a half-court zone defense. In this example, the guard brings the ball up the middle of the floor with the leftwing approximately ten feet behind the guard and about 15 feet to his right. The leftpost and rightwing are deep in the corners. The rightpost also starts deep in the lane area. The guard, as he approaches the midcourt line, passes back to the leftwing and then steps over the mid-court line to act as a safety. The leftwing dribbles across the ten-second line and the rightpost breaks to the high-point area, where he looks for an opening in the defense. The rightwing also moves out on the right sideline as a potential receiver. If the pass is successful in the middle, an immediate 3-on-2 situation exists. As one of the various options, the leftwing can pass to the rightwing who, in turn, passes to the rightpost rolling down the lane. The leftpost becomes another outlet for a pass as he breaks toward the basket.

Diagram 6-15 illustrates another half-court zone pressure option. This is our banana-series pattern explained in Chapter 4. In 6-15, the guard passes to the rightwing and then sets up across the

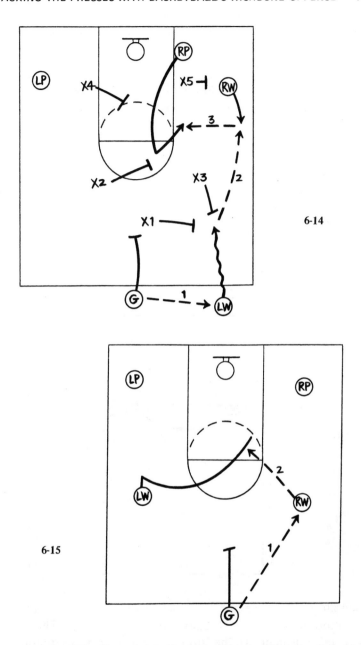

6-14

6-15

safety line as the outlet man. In this option, the rightwing passes to the leftwing who has broken in the clear in the middle area. The leftwing can now drive for the basket, pass off to either the rightpost or leftpost or reverse pivot and pass to the rightwing breaking as a trailer.

Attacking Man-to-Man Full-Court Pressure

Diagram 6-16 shows an option against man-to-man full-court pressure. Usually, we try to get the ball to our best dribbler and he brings the ball up the floor. We spend many hours of practice on just this one phase. This example depicts our slide pattern, in which the guard sets a screen on the wing and then rolls to the basket. The wing goes off the screen to the opposite corner.

Diagram 6-17 depicts our cross pattern. In this illustration, the guard and wing simply cross paths attempting to rub off their defensive men.

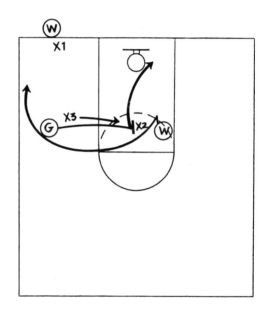

6-16

Diagram 6-18 shows one move when the defense puts two men on an inbounds receiver (usually our best dribbler). The defense usually takes a man off the inbounds passer in this situation. We instruct our players (in this case the guard) to simply step out of bounds and receive the pass across the endline. The guard then quickly returns the pass to the wing who has stepped in bounds.

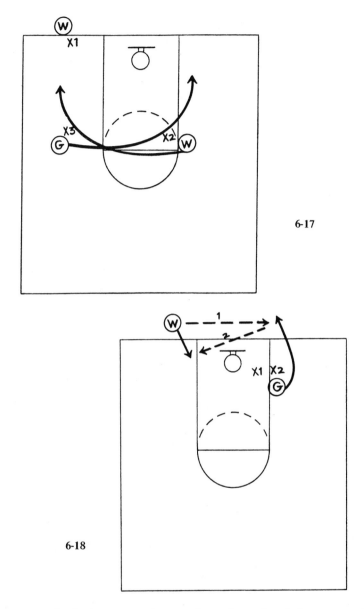

6-17

6-18

Diagram 6-19 shows another option when the defense uses the double-team. In this example, the guard breaks to the sideline clearing the middle for the postman, who breaks to the middle area. The postman can then bring the ball up or return the pass to the wing.

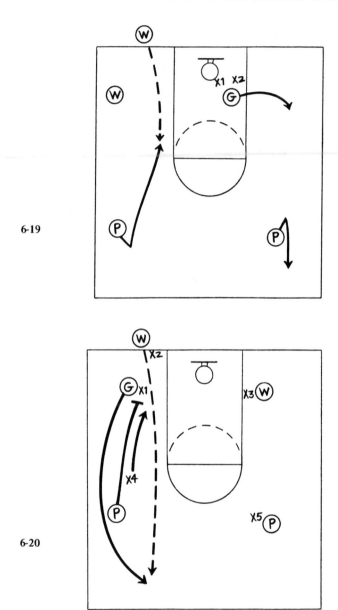

6-19

6-20

Diagram 6-20 shows another option we use versus man-to-man full-court pressure. In 6-20, the postman sets a screen on X1 and then rolls for the ball. The guard breaks long and is frequently open for the long pass if X4 doesn't switch to the guard.

We have also been successful in running our regular zone press offense as a man-to-man press offense for a "change of pace." (See Diagram 6-1.)

Attacking Man-to-Man Half-Court Pressure

Diagram 6-21 shows one of our options against a man-to-man half-court situation. We like to use short, fast passes, screens and rolls and drives. In 6-21, the guard passes to the rightwing. The wing looks for the trap, but quickly passes back to the guard and over to the leftwing. The rightwing then cuts down the middle for a pass and a drive. If there is no trap on the rightwing, he can dribble across into a trap and then pass to the leftpost, rightpost or leftwing, who breaks in the middle.

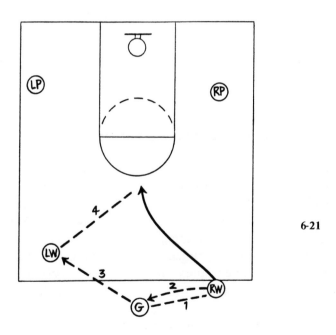

6-21

In Diagram 6-22, X2 has dropped off to double-team the guard. The rightwing simply breaks to an open area, yelling for the ball. Still another option would be for the rightwing (in 6-22) to come up and set a high screen on X2 and then immediately roll towards the basket as the guard dribbles around the screen.

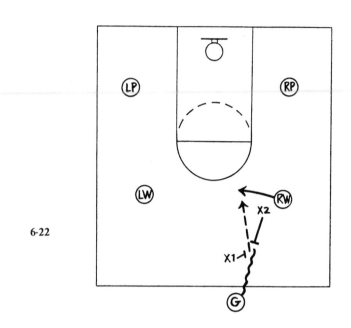

6-22

Tips for Defeating the Pressure Defenses

The following are our guidelines for beating the pressure defenses, and we drill these "tips" into our players daily:

1. Don't panic. Have confidence and poise. Whenever the defense has two men trapping, one offensive man has to be open. Stress positive thinking.
2. Expect to be double-teamed whenever you get the ball.
3. Break to the open spots and meet every pass. Practice moving toward the ball when receiving a pass. Never stand still!
4. Look for opportunities to split the trap or double-team.
5. Look for the press every time you take the ball out of bounds. This eliminates the surprise element.
6. Spread out the offense and try to use the weak side as much as possible. Try to force the defense to cover as

much of the court as possible. The weak-side man can often get open by simply breaking to the basket.

7. Never use a cross-court pass unless you are 100% sure of a completion. Never use a lob pass. Use short, snappy passes.
8. Ten seconds is a long time. Take your time and don't hurry unnecessarily. Don't try to go too fast.
9. We strive for vertical penetration on our passes. If a vertical pass is intercepted we have a better chance to cover up on defense.
10. Penetrate all the way to the endline if you can, but if the defense has "covered up," set up your regular offense. Don't take any wild or hurried shots.
11. Don't turn your back on a trap. The dribbler, if he is being double-teamed, should never turn his back to his own basket in back court.
12. Don't stand. Jockey and use good footwork to get open.
13. We designate one man to take the ball out of bounds each time. He should be able to know the "four-second" count and also be adept at bouncing the ball off a defensive man's leg in order to get another chance to throw the ball into play.
14. We practice every day against the press in some form.
15. Each player must know the approximate positions of his teammates.
16. Move along the endline to find the most advantageous spot at which to throw the ball in. Never pass from underneath the backboard.
17. If you are breaking to an area and you find it covered by a defensive man, quickly break to the nearest open area.
18. Never try to dribble unless you have ample room to do so.
19. Potential receivers of the inbounds pass should never allow themselves to be pinned too close to the baseline or sideline prior to meeting the pass. Start your move a little closer to the mid-court area. If the double-team gets you in a trap near the sideline, the defense actually has four men on you, counting the two court lines.
20. Never cluster in one area; spread out.
21. Don't pass just to get rid of the ball. Pass to the closest open man.

22. Frequently, the player taking ball out-of-bounds should fake a first pass with his eyes, or with an arm pump.
23. Maintain good balance when you receive a pass so you will be able to make a good move.
24. Players should learn to fake a pass from all positions on the floor. A fake pass normally "freezes" a press momentarily.
25. Players in possession of the ball should always expect pressure from behind when the ball has broken by the front line of a press.
26. If at all possible, never leave a ball-handling teammate alone in the backcourt. This is drilled in our three-across pattern (Diagram 6-11).
27. Take a jump ball (a five-second count) in a pressure situation rather than throw the ball away.
28. Keep your head up. Don't look down at the floor.
29. Avoid crosses near the ball to prevent trapping.
30. Pass and go away. Keep the defense spread among teammates, but move in closer if they need help.
31. Isolate the good dribbler and let him bring the ball up against man-to-man pressure. Hold dribbling to a minimum against a zone press.

Our Favorite Press-Offense Drills

1. THREE IN THE RING (See Diagram 6-23)

This drill teaches a player to pass under pressure. The coaches toss a ball to one of the players, in this diagram, number one. Players eight, nine and ten are in the middle. The two players in the center, in this case, nine and ten, who are closest to number one, double-team him. Number one tries to pass to anyone in the circle, but he cannot pass to the two beside him, players two and seven. Number eight tries to intercept and, if he does, or if he gets his hand on the ball, he replaces player one and one goes into the middle.

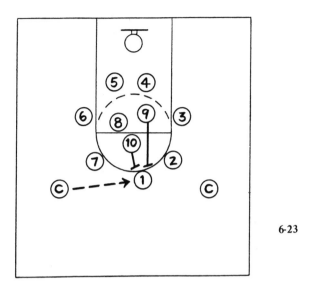

6-23

2. TWO-VERSUS-EIGHT DRILL (See Diagram 6-24)

G and W try to advance the ball the length of the court through the four areas. The two defensive men in each area try to steal the ball. They may play defense only in their area. The players rotate with the two X's in area one, going on offense, and the other X's move up one area. The G and W take over defensive positions in area four.

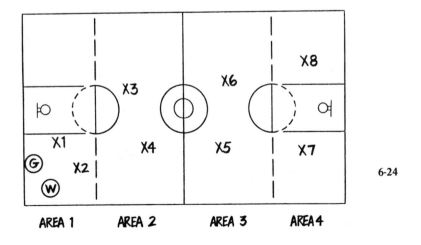

6-24

3. PASSING AND RECEIVING DRILL (See Diagram 6-25)

Player one passes to two or three. If the pass is completed, the receiver pivots and passes to his teammate breaking down court. X1 tries to make player two throw a bad pass.

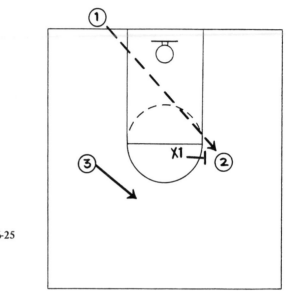

6-25

4. NO-BOUNCE DRILL

You run your press offense and no player can put the ball on the floor, except for a bounce pass. Dribbling is a violation. Through this drill, players learn to pass the ball upcourt and players without the ball learn the importance of getting free into receiving positions. As a variation, we also run this drill with our dribble blinders (glasses) on.

5. COMPETITION DRILL

Team A takes the ball down the floor and Team B presses. When Team A makes a violation or scores, Team B gets the ball and goes against Team A's defense. If the defensive team steals the ball, they still get the ball on offense in their regular turn, regardless of whether they score or not.

The winner is the first team to score 21 points, and points are scored in the following manner:

1 point basket
1 point free throw (every foul a one-and-one)
1 point steal
1 point each time you cross the timeline successfully

6. SEVEN-ON-FIVE DRILL

We run our press offense against seven defensive players. We find this drill helps to build confidence, because the players realize that if they can defeat seven defensive players, they should have an easier time beating five. We have also added an eighth player on defense in some situations.

7.

Coordinating Basketball's
Wishbone with
Special-Situation Plays

In this chapter we will describe our "special" out-of-bounds plays, jump-ball specials, length-of-court specials, fast-break patterns from the free throw and, finally, our Wishbone-Offense patterns versus the various combination defenses.

All of the special play situations in this chapter have been tested by the author and have met with success. The reader may have a genuine interest in our out-of-bounds and jump-ball plays, which are definitely unorthodox, and some coaches may call it "unheard of." Other coaches are afraid to use such tactics for fear of failure and criticism. We call it "adding a little color and fun to the game," and our players react the same way. Most importantly, we are trying to win games fairly and within the rules.

If the special-situation play is successful, it always seems to disrupt and injure the morale of our opponents for a few minutes. As a warning, however, if the play doesn't work, your fans may want to run for the tar and feathers! We always prepare our players mentally for these occasions by telling them that there is a definite possibility that the play may not work. We do not want to suffer a letdown in team morale if the "sure" basket is lost.

We must point out that we do have our regular series of out-of-bounds and jump-ball plays and that the plays listed in this chapter are used only on rare or "special" occasions. On all of our plays we run a safety outlet, so if the sure basket is not available, we still retain possession of the ball.

Out-of-Bounds Plays Underneath

The *I'll Take It Out* play is shown in Diagram 7-1. The players line up in a box formation with players two and three lining up high, approximately 12 feet from the basket. As player one snaps the ball in his hand to initiate the play, player two steps forward and says loudly, "Hey hold it—I'll take the ball out!" He has his hands at his sides and he starts in toward player one as if he is going to take the ball out of bounds. Player one, also carrying out the fake, quickly gives a pass to player two, who has suddenly cut from the basket for an easy layup.

As a variation, player three can say, "Wait a second—Joe (player two) takes the ball out," and then Joe moves in for the basket. Player five goes to the right corner after faking left and becomes a safety. Player four is the deep safety. As in all other plays in this section, this can be started from either side of the floor.

We scored 14 baskets in one season off this play, and we have also had several three-point plays result, as the defense sometimes adjusts in time to foul. However, this type of play has its drawbacks. In one game, we were losing by two points with one second on the clock. We worked the play to perfection and our player had an unmolested layup—which he missed! On another occasion one of our players was so stunned at his wide-open layup opportunity, he fumbled the ball out of bounds. As you can see, this type of play takes great acting and timing to perform.

The *Smash Em* play is diagramed in 7-2. The players line up as diagramed with players two and three approximately 20 feet apart. As player one snaps the ball to start the play, players two and three head for each other as fast as possible and, faking a collision, both players sprawl to the floor. Player four is the safety outlet, and he fakes right and then goes deep to the left side of the floor. Player five breaks high as players two and three are moving

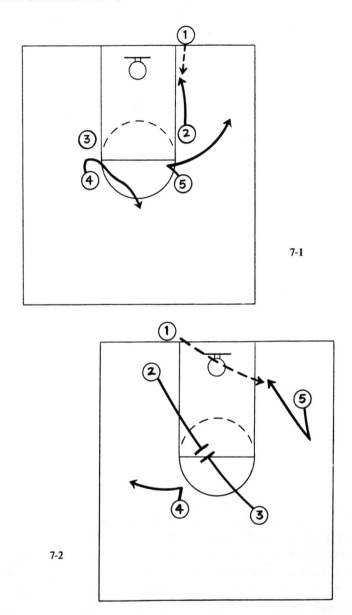

7-1

7-2

towards each other and, as the collision unfolds, player five quickly reverses and is often wide open for a layup as all of the defensive players usually watch the "collision." This has also been used as a side out-of-bounds pattern.

Diagram 7-3 illustrates our *Dummy* play. Player three is being guarded by X1 and is facing player one. X1 cannot see the ball because he is hooking directly at three with his hands up. Player three dummys X1 into thinking he is not going to get the ball. He must remain expressionless and motionless, giving the appearance of not being involved in the play. Player one passes to three and, as the ball passes over X1's head, three moves his hands up quickly and catches the ball for a quick basket.

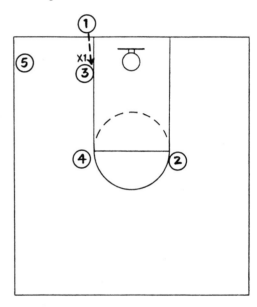

7-3

Diagram 7-4 depicts our *Bounceback* play. You have the same situation as in the dummy play in Diagram 7-3. In this sequence, player one bounces the ball off X1's back and then quickly jumps inbounds for an easy basket. This perfectly legal play had an important part in an overtime upset victory when I coached in Indiana. With a minute and a half remaining and the score tied in overtime, we were given the opportunity to use the bounceback. The result was a surprisingly easy basket, which seemed to completely demoralize our opponents. We reeled off ten more points for a 12-point overtime victory.

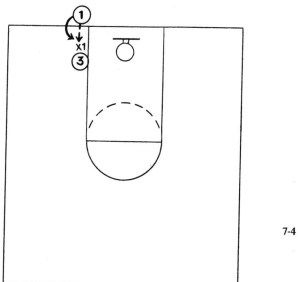

7-4

Diagram 7-5 illustrates our *Cartwheel* play. The players line up in the box formation. As player one snaps the ball to initiate the play, players two, four and five do a gymnastic stunt on the floor, such as a cartwheel. (In one game our players did a forward roll.) As the three players on the floor are cartwheeling, player three starts moving high and then reverses quickly for an easy basket, as the defense becomes awed by the stunts. Player four cartwheels into a safety position and the other players break from their cartwheel positions, being sure to leave the right area open for player three. This play can also be used as a side out-of-bounds pattern.

As a variation of the cartwheel and smash em' plays, you can achieve the same effect by having one of your players fall to the floor and fake an injury. We have never used this one—and we never will.

Diagram 7-6 depicts our *Join Hands* play. The legality of this play has been questioned, but I have been unable to find a rule-book statement declaring this play illegal. We used this play

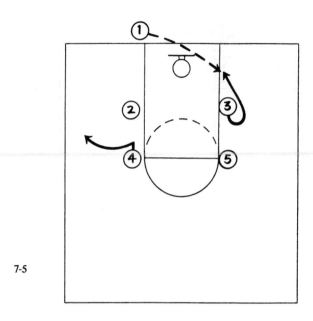

7-5

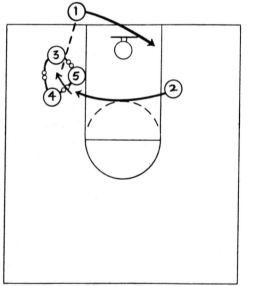

7-6

three times in my early years of coaching and we garnered three baskets! As player one snaps the ball, players three, four and five join hands in a circle, and player two runs into the circle (three,

four and five allow him in). Player two usually has an unmolested
bank shot. Player four then becomes the safety outlet.

Sideline Out-of-Bounds Plays

Diagram 7-7 shows our *Backboard* play. Player one snaps the
ball to start the play and then throws the ball off the backboard.
This is more difficult than it sounds, and it requires much practice.
As player one snaps the ball, player four screens five and five
breaks to the basket for a possible carom off the backboard.
Player two screens three and three breaks to the basket on the left
side. Players four and two roll off their screens for safety outlets.
Player one drops back on defense. The defense often becomes
stunned and will freeze momentarily as the ball hits the
backboard, thinking that this is accidental.

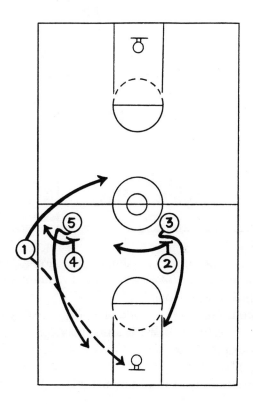

7-7

Diagram 7-8 illustrates our *Wrongway* play. You have the ball out-of-bounds with your offensive basket to the right. (This play always works best after a time out.) Instruct your players to line up facing the basket at the left (your opponent's offensive basket) as if you were going for that basket. The player taking the ball out (player one) faces the basket at the left also. You will be surprised at how many times the defense will line up in good defensive position—at their own offensive basket!

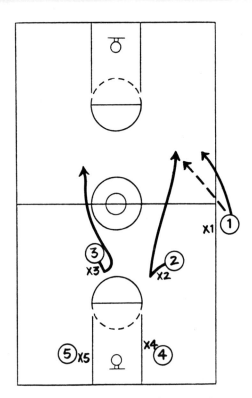

7-8

As player one slaps the ball player two simply fakes going deep and then reverses to the other end of the floor for an unmolested shot. Players one and three trail the play.

Diagram 7-9 depicts our *Eat Up the Clock* play. (The legality of this play has also been questioned.) We use this play, of course, when we want to run out the clock. We also have options that can turn this into a scoring play. Players two, three, four and five line up as shown, in a special side out-of-bounds play. They are shoulder-to-shoulder with their backs to the ball. On the slap of the ball by player one, the players turn quickly facing the ball and remain shoulder-to-shoulder. Player one passes to either three or four in the middle of the "wall." Players three and four simply hand the ball back and forth until the clock runs out or until they are fouled.

In one game, we used this play with a one point lead and six seconds left on the clock. Finally, as time was running out, X2 came around to the out-of-bounds side to try to break up the play. When this happens, as soon as player two sees X2 going to break up the play, he simply turns and goes full speed for the basket.

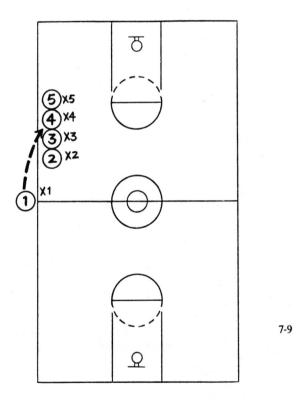

7-9

Jump-Ball Specials

Diagram 7-10 illustrates our *Crazy* jump-ball play. Player one tips the ball to either two or three, who dribbles across the center line going towards the wrong basket. Players four and five break hard in the wrong direction, carrying out the decoy action. In 7-10, player three stops and reverse pivots and passes to player one, who has hesitated and then broken in the proper direction.

Diagram 7-11 shows our *Double Tip* play. Player one tips the ball to player two, who jumps up in the air and, without catching the ball, tips the ball back to player five, who has broken long off player three's screen. This is a play that demands much practice and timing.

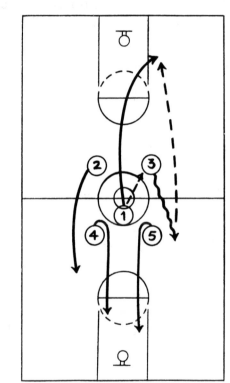

7-10

Length-of-the-Court Plays

Our length-of-the-court plays are shown in Diagrams 7-12 and 7-13. In Diagram 7-12, as player one slaps the ball to initiate the play, player two steps out of bounds also. Player one passes along the endline to player two. Player three screens player one's

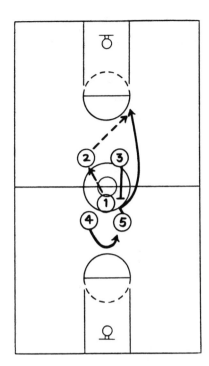

7-11

7-12

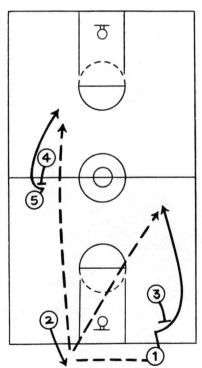

defensive man and player four screens five's defensive man. Two passes to either one or five. Remember, the clock does not start until the ball touches a player in-bounds.

In Diagram 7-13, player one again passes to player two, who has stepped out-of-bounds. Player one then goes long at a full burst of speed. Players four and five break across the lane. Player three loops to the left side and deep. Player five, on his break, sets a screen on player one's defensive man. Two passes long to one or three on the sideline. Often, player one will be wide open.

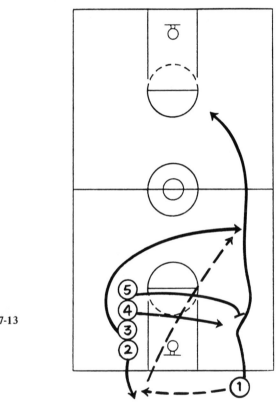

7-13

Free-Throw Fast-Break Specials

Our free-throw fast-break specials are depicted in Diagrams 7-14, 7-15 and 7-16. We have used the following setups to get

3-on-2, 3-on-1 and 4-on-2 situations and have scored many quick baskets. In Diagram 7-14, player two "rebounds" the successful free throw and, if he is right-handed, will normally take the ball out-of-bounds on the right side. Players three and four are in the mid-court area and player five is in the far left corner. Player five should be a good corner shooter as he will receive numerous scoring opportunities.

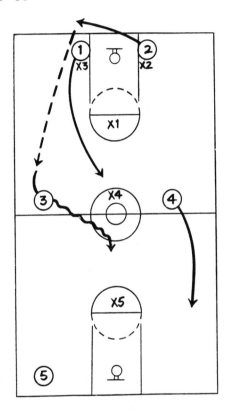

7-14

Player two steps out-of-bounds quickly after the free throw is made and passes to player three, who breaks to meet the ball. Player three goes to the middle of the floor immediately and joins four and five in a fast-break situation. If done quickly, there should be an automatic one-man advantage and a possible two-man advantage. X1, the free-throw shooter, will often become so intent upon getting back on defense he will not concentrate and miss the free throw.

If the free throw is missed and the rebound goes to the right side, player number four will break up for the quick outlet pass and then immediately head for the middle. Player three breaks down the left side and player five crosses over to the right corner.

In Diagram 7-15, we line up with players one and two in rebound position and player three in position to screen the shooter temporarily. Players four and five go deep to the right and left corners. If the free throw is missed and bounces to the right side and is rebounded by player two, he quickly gives an outlet pass to player three. Player three screens the shooter and then breaks to the side of the rebound. Player three then dribbles quickly to the middle or, if covered, passes to player one, who cuts quickly to the middle if he sees that player three is covered. Players four and five are in opposite corners looking for a fast-break advantage.

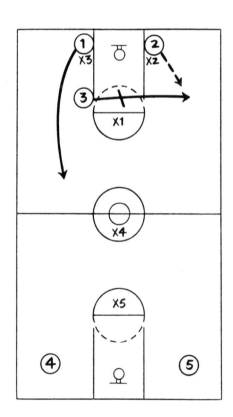

7-15

If the free throw is successful, player two takes the ball out-of-bounds quickly and passes to player three, who has broken quickly to the left side. As soon as three sees that the free throw is good, he makes his sprint. Player one breaks up the middle as a trailer or for a quick side pass if three is covered by a defensive man, in this case, probably X4.

Diagram 7-16 illustrates another fast-break pattern as players one, two and three line up the same way as in Diagram 7-15. Players four and five line up in the mid-court area. If the free throw is successful, player one takes the ball out-of-bounds quickly and passes to three, who has screened the shooter X1 and then broken to the left side. Player three now looks for player five, who has crossed with player four and is breaking to the left side. Player four goes down the middle and player two comes down the weak side to make the quick break, with player three as the trailer.

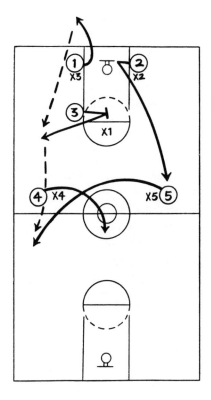

7-16

If the free throw is unsuccessful and player one or two rebounds, he immediately passes to the side of the rebound to player three. Player three has again screened the shooter and has broken to the rebound side.

Wishbone Offense Versus the Combination Defenses

For purposes of variety, all play patterns in this section will originate on the left side of the court. (All patterns in previous chapters have begun on the right side.) Again, the play patterns can be run to either side of the floor with equal effectiveness. All Wishbone play patterns have worked against the combination defenses. Some will work better for some teams than they will for others. For the sake of brevity, we have listed just one play pattern example for each defense.

Wishbone Versus the Match-Up Defenses

The match-up defenses we have encountered are of two types: zone and man-to-man in origin. In the first type, the defense lines up in a zone and then picks up the offense man-to-man on the first pass. In the second type, the defense lines up man-to-man with the offense and then uses zone principles. For example, when facing the Wishbone Offense, our opponents would line up in a 1-2-2, man-to-man defense.

Teams playing against this defense should not congest areas away from the ball where one defensive man can guard two offensive men. You should also try to omit inside screens. Diagonal cuts make trading of men (essential in the match-up) difficult and they confuse the defense.

We have found the Wishbone Offense to be very effective against both types of match-up defense. However, the inside screens on the give-and-go screen and the block-and-roll have proved very ineffective. Usually, the rule of the match-up defense is to let offensive cutters go on through if they are taking a path away from the ball. We have found it advantageous to speed up our offense, and this gives more problems to the defense as they have to make faster decisions in selecting their man to guard.

We ran into a match-up defense in a recent sectional championship game against Hampshire High School. We ran the baseline
series and block-and-roll pattern (minus the sideline screen)
exclusively the first half and we led 32 to 18, canning 14 of 22
field-goal attempts.

WISHBONE VERSUS THE BOX-AND-ONE

Diagram 7-17 illustrates the Wishbone Offense against the
box-and-one defense with the "hawk" on the lonesome guard. In
7-17, the wingman-cutback pattern is being run to the left side.
X1, X2, X3 and X4 play in a box-zone formation while X5 is the
hawk on the guard, going man-to-man at all times. In this example,
the guard passes to the leftwing and the leftwing looks inside the
zone for the rightwing, who has faked downward and then come
back looking for an opening in the zone. All of the options of the
wingman-cutback pattern are available. The reader should refer to
Chapter 2 to review all the options of the wingman-cutback
pattern.

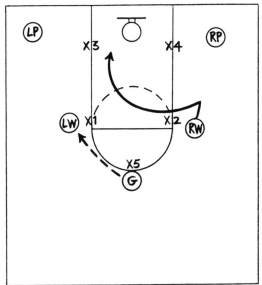

7-17

Diagram 7-18 depicts the Wishbone against the box-and-one
with the hawk on the wingman. In this example, the hawk, X5, is
guard the rightwing man-to-man with the other four defensive men

in the box zone. The block-and-roll pattern is being run. The leftwing sets a wide screen on X1 and the guard drives off the screen. Often the guard will have an easy jump shot or, if X3 comes high to pick up the guard, the leftwing will be open on the roll. All of the options of the block-and-roll pattern are available. The reader should refer to Chapter 3 to review all the options of the block-and-roll.

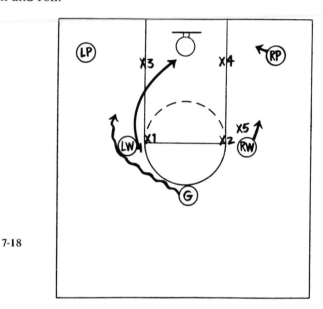

7-18

The box-and-one and diamond-and-one defenses are basically the same after the initial pass has been made. The primary use of the two defenses is to limit the effectiveness of a high-scoring player.

WISHBONE OFFENSE VERSUS THE DIAMOND-AND-ONE

Diagram 7-19 depicts the postman-roll pattern versus the diamond-and-one defense. The X1, X2, X3 and X4 defensive players are in a diamond zone formation while the hawk, X5 is on the rightpost man-to-man. The guard passes to the leftwing and the leftpost sets a screen on X2. The leftwing often has an easy jumper or sometimes a drive to the basket. If X4 picks up the leftwing, the leftpost has a big advantage on his quick roll to the basket. All of the options of the postman-roll pattern are available.

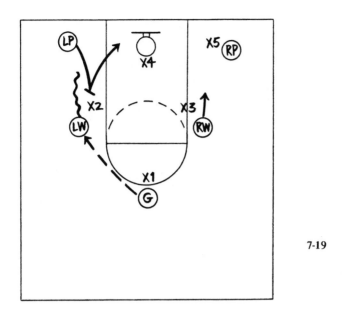

7-19

Diagram 7-20 illustrates the lonesome-guard reverse pattern against a diamond-and-one zone with the hawk on the wing. Often, the guard is open on his cut down the middle and the leftwing has the additional option of passing to the leftpost low or to the guard in his move to the left corner. X2 and X4 have big adjustment problems. All of the options of the lonesome-guard reverse pattern are available. The reader should refer to Chapter 3 to review all the options of the lonesome-guard reverse.

WISHBONE OFFENSE VERSUS THE T-AND-ONE

Diagram 7-21 illustrates our give-and-go screen pattern against a T-and-one zone with the hawk on the rightwing. X2, X3, X4 and X5 set up in a T formation with X1 as the hawk on the rightwing. The leftwing takes the pass from the guard and then passes to the leftpost. Very often the leftwing will be open on his quick cut to the basket as X4 covers the corner. All of the options of the give-and-go screen pattern are available.

WISHBONE OFFENSE VERSUS THE TRIANGLE-PLUS-TWO

Diagram 7-22 depicts our baseline series against the triangle-

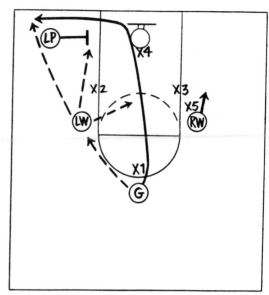

7-20

7-21

and-two defense. In this defense two defenders, X1 and X2, play
man-to-man against the top two offensive players while X3, X4
and X5 play a zone in triangle fashion. In this example the
baseline series is immediately set up with the rightwing having the

initial options of passing to the rightpost low or the leftwing in the corner. All of the options of the baseline series are available.

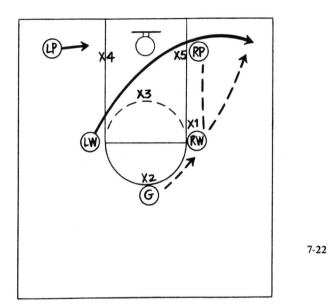

7-22

W ISHBONE OFFENSE VERSUS THE 3-MEN MAN-TO-MAN

Diagram 7-23 shows our block-and-roll play pattern against a two-man zone with three players in a man-to-man defense. Two defenders, X4 and X5, play a zone while X1, X2 and X3 play their opponents man-to-man. The leftwing sets a wide screen on X1. All the options of the block-and-roll pattern are available.

WISHBONE OFFENSE VERSUS THE 3-MAN ZONE

Diagram 7-24 illustrates our postman-roll pattern against a three-man zone and the two back players, X5 and X4, are man-to-man. X1, X2 and X3 are in a triangle zone in front. The leftwing often has an easy shot off the leftpost's screen or the leftpost is open on his roll to the basket. All of the options of the postman-roll pattern are available.

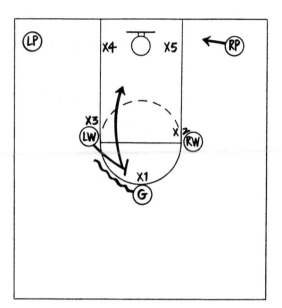

7-23

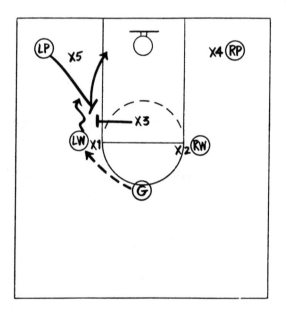

7-24

8.

Developing Offensive
Fundamentals for
Basketball's Wishbone

The offensive fundamental drills described in this chapter are concentrated in the ball-handling areas, which include passing, receiving and dribbling. Also, a couple of our favorite offensive footwork drills are listed. A few of our ball-handling drills are listed in other sections of this book. Two examples are the Eleven-Man Drill (Diagram 1-5) and the Elgin Eleven (pages 28-30) described in Chapter 1. Our field-goal and free-throw shooting drills are described in Chapters 9 and 10.

I believe that fundamentals and team spirit are the two most important things in the development of a successful team. Teams that have been well-drilled in fundamentals will usually have a great degree of confidence, and good ball-handling teams are hard to beat.

One of the cardinal sins in the game of basketball is to lose possession of the ball without getting a good shot at the basket. Few field goals are scored without one or more passes setting up the shot attempt and nothing makes a team look worse than poor ball handling. Drills should be designed for a specific purpose and they should comprise a part of your offense. Also, it is necessary to work on a specific fundamental rather than to develop a part of your offense.

Sound individual fundamentals are synonymous with sound habits of team play. Passing is the foundation of scoring, and the art of passing is second only to that of shooting. Passing is made up of several key elements, among which are timing, peripheral vision, quick hands and a good head for the game. Poor shooting teams must necessarily be fine passing teams in order to work the ball in closer to the basket.

The dribble has an important place in basketball. Some of the uses of the dribble are:

1. To advance the ball upcourt.
2. To drive through defensive openings for scoring.
3. To protect a lead and the ball in the final part of a game.
4. To escape pressing tactics (especially man-to-man).
5. To clear an area after rebounding.
6. To get out of trouble if a teammate cannot free himself for a pass.

Rookie players tend to waste their dribble by bouncing the ball aimlessly as soon as they obtain possession. A player who has used up his dribble is stopped from further advancement; a player who still has his dribble is alive. So never waste your dribble!

If a coach were to check his game statistics closely he would find that many of the loss-of-possession errors are caused by poor receiving rather than poor passing. Good receivers must catch passes thrown from many angles and at various speeds.

The coach must have the patience to drill and drill and drill some more. Each player should have an opportunity for correct performance of the fundamental skills of the game. A good team is one that is sound—fundamentally.

1. FIVE-CORNER DRILL

The five-corner drill (Diagram 8-1) requires the player to meet the pass, pass quickly, and then move to a new corner following his pass. This is a good pregame warm-up drill. The players line up as illustrated in Diagram 8-1 and pass the ball with two-handed chest passes. The players are approximately 12-15 feet apart.

Player one passes to player two and follows his pass behind player two's corner. Player two passes to player three and follows his pass behind player three's corner. Player three passes to player four and follows his pass behind player four's corner. Player four passes to player five, etc. Player five completes the cycle by passing to player one, etc. This drill continues in this manner with the players slowly closing the gap from 12-15 feet to approximately five feet apart.

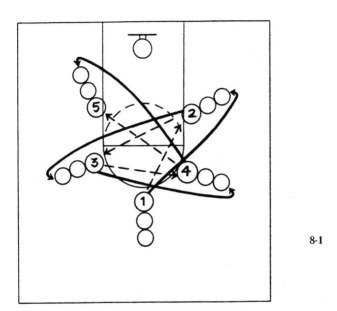

8-1

2. FOUR-CORNER DRILL

The four-corner drill (Diagram 8-2) again requires the player to meet the pass, pass quickly and then follow his pass. The team is divided into four squads. The first player in squad one passes to the first player in squad two, squad two passes to squad three, squad three to squad four and, finally completing the cycle, squad four to squad one.

You can alter the drill by having the passers go to the opposite corner of the corner to which they have passed the ball.

3. CHAIN-PASSING DRILL

The chain-passing drill (Diagram 8-3) is noted for having the players meet the pass and for making the players pass quickly and accurately.

The team is divided into two squads facing each other about 15 feet apart. The first player in squad one passes to the first player in squad two. The player in squad two receives the ball and then gives a short flip pass to player one, who is breaking towards two's line. Player one then gives a short flip pass to the second player in squad two.

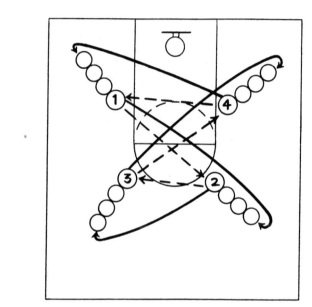

8-2

4. TWO-LINES PASSING DRILL

The two-lines passing drill affords each player ample work on all kinds of passes in just a short time. The drill starts with the team divided into two squads with each pair of players having a ball and passing at a distance of approximately eight feet or more, using the proper techniques. The pairs of players gradually move further apart. We use the following passes in this drill: two-hand chest pass; two-hand bounce pass; two-hand overhead pass; step-and-flip pass; baseball pass.

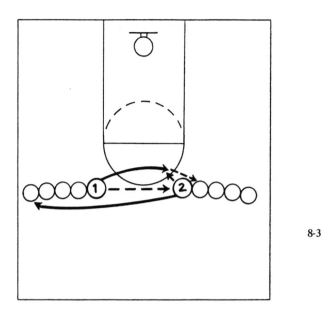

8-3

5. HALF-COURT BASEBALL-PASS DRILL

This is a good drill for stressing timing and execution. The team is divided into two squads as in Diagram 8-4. The two squads line up parallel to each other at the mid-court line. The first player in line one dribbles toward the sideline with the first player in line two cutting behind and downcourt. Player one throws a well-timed baseball pass that can be taken by player two at approximately the free-throw circle for a layup. Player one goes behind player two's line and player two behind one's line, and they exchange responsibilities.

6. MACHINE-GUN DRILL

The machine-gun drill, illustrated in Diagram 8-5, is excellent for developing side or peripheral vision. Players get into squads of six players. One player in each group is about ten feet in the middle of the players and facing them. Two balls are used. As the player facing the line passes to any member of the five-player line, the other ball is passed to him. The two balls are then moved continuously up and down the line. The players then rotate positions with each player getting the opportunity to be the "it" man.

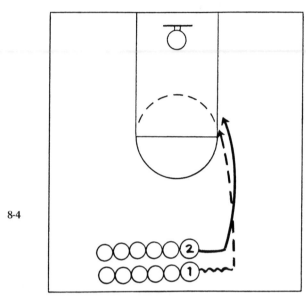

8-4

8-5

7. TEAM ROLL-BALL DRILL

This drill, depicted in Diagram 8-6, offers practice in developing many skills. A player must hustle and scrap for the ball with his teammate; he must develop the ability to scoop the ball while on the move and then regain his balance; and it affords good one-on-one offensive work. It also requires aggressiveness and quick reactions.

The team is divided into two squads and the two teams are in single file on the end line facing the other end of the court. The coach is in the middle on the end line. The players in both lines look straight ahead and not back at the coach. The coach rolls the ball to some area on the court and both players from each line hustle after it. The player who retrieves the ball is then the offensive man and the other player goes on defense.

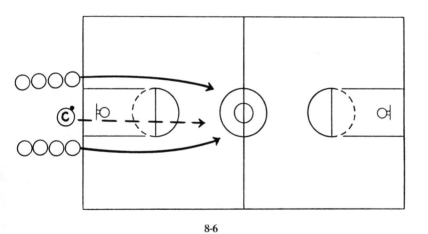

8-6

The game goes to 20 points. Points are scored as follows: one point for each time the ball is retrieved; two points for a basket; and if a player is fouled, he shoots a one-and-bonus free throw.

8. STEAL-THE-BACON DRILL

This drill, illustrated in Diagram 8-7, offers the same basic skills as in the team roll-ball drill. The team is divided into two squads with the two squads on opposite sidelines approximately 40 feet apart.

Each line counts off with each player having a corresponding number in each line. The coach rolls the ball between the lines and then calls a number. The players in each line whose numbers have been called hustle to the ball. The player who retrieves the ball tries to score as the other player goes on defense.

The game goes to 20 points. Scoring is two points for each basket and, if a player is fouled, he shoots a one-and-bonus free throw. The coach can call two, three or four numbers at once, thus offering two-on-two, three-on-three, and other situations.

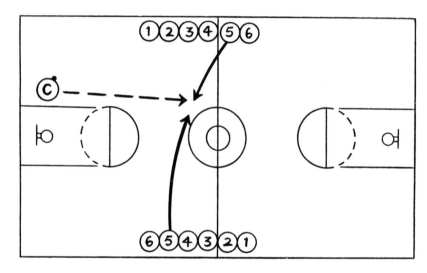

8-7

9. TWO-BALL BULL-IN-THE-RING DRILL

The two-ball bull-in-the-ring drill, shown in Diagram 8-8, has players six and seven acting as the "bulls" in the middle of the circle. Two balls are used. The players in the circle cannot pass to the men immediately next to them. The circle has six players. Consider the ball a "hot" object that has to be moved quickly. If one of the "bulls" touches the ball or intercepts a pass, the passer exchanges places with him.

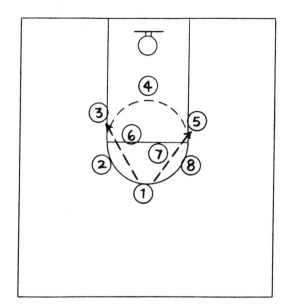

8-8

10. TWO-MAN TWO-BALL DRILL

This drill is excellent for ball handling. The squad divides into groups of two. Players one and two have basketballs. The players pass to each other as quickly as possible making the passes extremely accurate. The balls must be passed on different levels; for example, if player one is using a two-hand overhead pass, player two must use a chest pass or bounce pass. The players are spaced about 20 feet apart.

11. THREE-LINE FIGURE-EIGHT DRILL

This drill is one of the oldest in basketball and is great for timing and accurate passing to a moving target. The team is divided into squads of three in single file on the end line. The player in the middle line (first player) passes to his right to the first player in the third line, who has broken onto the court. The passer always goes behind the player he has passed to. The first player in the third line, who has just received the pass, passes to the first player in the first line. Again, the passer always cuts behind the receiver. The first player in the first line, who has just received the pass, now completes the cycle by passing to the middle player again. This is a continuous drill, run to the far end of the floor and back, and then the next trio of players go.

As a variation, we use a medicine ball first and then a basketball.

12. LEFTHANDED BASKETBALL

This is a drill to strengthen the "weak" hand. Divide the team into squads of five players. Play two teams at each basket. A weak-handed game is played with the players committing a violation anytime the right hand is used. Of course, if the player is lefthanded he uses only his right hand.

13. HEADS-UP DRIBBLE DRILL

Our heads-up dribble drill is illustrated in Diagram 8-9. This is an excellent drill for teaching the players to keep their heads up while dribbling and not to watch the ball. The team is divided into two squads and the two squads go to opposite ends of the floor. Chairs are placed on the floor approximately 12 feet apart. (Towels can be substituted for chairs.)

On a signal from the coach, the first player in each line starts weaving around the chairs. If the players do not keep their heads up there is a definite danger of a collision. The two players then go to the ends of their opposite lines.

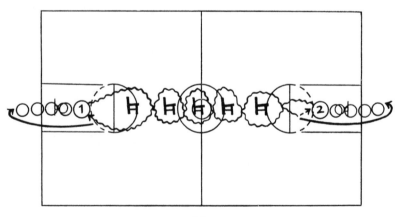

8-9

14. HOLLYWOOD DRILL

The team is divided into three squads and they line up on the end line in single file. The first player in each squad dribbles to the mid-court line and back and then hands off to the next player in line. During his dribble to the mid-court line, each player must dribble behind his back, between his legs, with his left and right hands, etc.

15. DRIBBLE-SPEED RELAY DRILL

The team is divided into groups of two and the players line up on the end line. The first player in each group dribbles to the opposite end line and back and gives the ball to his teammate, who repeats the process. Each team goes three continuous times.

We also have the players do the same drill using only their "weak" hand.

16. DRIBBLE TAG

This drill is a good conditioner, and it teaches the players to keep their heads and eyes up while dribbling. The entire squad is placed in the half-court area with the out-of-bounds lines serving as boundaries. One player is given the ball and is declared "it." He must dribble the ball and chase the other members of the team until he catches and tags someone. As an added stipulation, he must be in control of the ball at the moment of the tag.

17. CIRCLE DRIBBLE, PIVOT, PASS DRILL

This drill, as depicted in Diagram 8-10, helps to teach dribbling, pivoting and passing. The team is divided into four squads and two balls are used. The players are approximately 25 feet apart. A ball is given to the first player in squads two and four.

The players dribble to the middle, plant their right foot and pivot, facing the squad on their right. The first players in squads one and three receive the passes and then repeat the process. The player follows his pass to the end of the line. As a variation, you can have the players pass and pivot to their left.

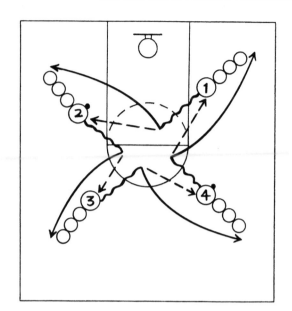

8-10

18. DRIBBLE INDIVIDUAL GAME DRILL

Five players are in a circle, each with a basketball. On a signal from the coach, each player tries to knock the ball of one of his opponents out of the circle while dribbling the ball. Play is continued until one player remains, and he is declared the winner. Then have the winners play off for the individual team championship. This drill teaches the player to protect the ball with his body.

19. DRIBBLE-CHAIRS RELAY

The dribble-chairs relay is illustrated in Diagram 8-11. This drill teaches the players to keep their heads up while dribbling and also the art of shooting a layup under high-speed pressure. The team is divided into two squads. Three chairs are lined up across the parallel of the free-throw line. Each team has a ball. Players one and two start to dribble, weaving around the chairs. Each player rebounds his own shot and passes to the second man in line. The first team to score 15 baskets is the winner. Again, as in the heads-up dribble drill diagrammed in 8-9, if the players do not keep their heads up there is a good possibility of a collision.

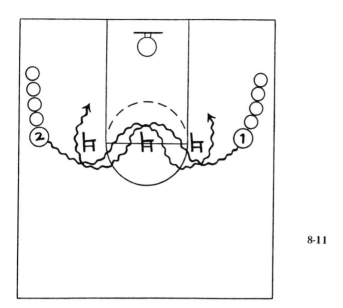

8-11

20. OBSTACLE-LINE DRILL

The obstacle-line drill is depicted in Diagram 8-12. Five or six players form a stationary obstacle line approximately five feet apart. The remaining players form a line facing these players. Player one dribbles in and out, changing hands, weaving through the five X players. Players in the X line may wave their arms or try to steal the ball by slapping at it, but must remain stationary.

21. TWO-BALL INDIVIDUAL-RELAY DRILL

The team divides into two squads. Each player dribbles to the end line with two basketballs, one for each hand. This drill is much more difficult to perform than it appears, especially under relay conditions. It takes excellent timing and good fingertip control. If the player loses control of either ball, he starts over. Each team goes twice and the first team to finish is the winner.

22. POOR-PASS DRILL

This drill teaches receivers to be alert for movements in any direction. The team divides into groups of two. There is one ball for each group. The players are approximately 15 feet apart. The players purposely pass high, low or wide to each other.

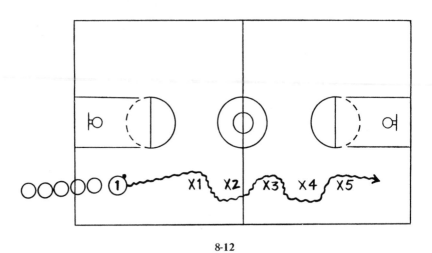

8-12

23. TWO-BALL PICKUP DRILL

This is a drill to teach timing and good balance in scooping a ball and shooting a power layup. The drill is illustrated in Diagram 8-13. The B stands for a basketball. At the coach's signal, player one hustles in picks up the ball and puts it in the basket. He then picks up the ball on the opposite side of the lane and puts it in the basket. While player one is putting the second ball in the basket, player X3 is retrieving the first ball and placing it back on the floor in its original position. The player continues this drill back and forth for 30 seconds. Then the three players rotate positions. A player should be able to make 16 baskets in a 30-second time period.

24. PIVOT-AND-CATCH DRILL

This drill helps to develop quickness and coordination. The team divides into groups of two. Player one has the ball and player two is 15 feet away with his back to player one. Player one slaps the ball and this is the signal for player two to turn and quickly face the ball. The ball should be in the air as player two is turning. Player one should throw the ball hard and at all angles.

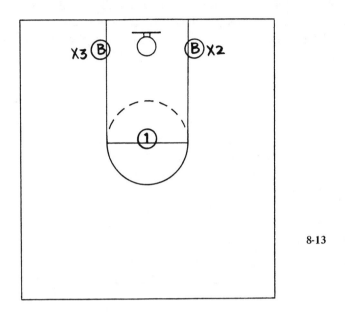

8-13

25. FOUR-LINES, FOUR-BALLS DRILL

This drill is good for teaching timing, accurate passing and receiving. The team divides into four squads. The squads go to four corners as in the four-corner drill in Diagram 8-2. The squads are approximately 15-18 feet apart; each squad has a basketball. On signal from the coach, the first player in each squad dribbles to the middle, pivots and passes to the second man in line. The drill can be run right or left.

26. HALF-COURT DRILL (NO DRIBBLE)

This drill eliminates dribbling entirely and is played only on half of the court. The team is divided into groups of three, four or five players and can be played three-on-three, four-on-four or five-on-five, depending on the amount of available players and baskets. The teams play a regular scrimmage with only shooting and passing allowed—no dribbling!

27. BACKWARD-RUNNING DRILL

All players line up on the end line. At the coach's signal, the players sprint backwards the length of the court and then return. Repeat 10-15 times. This helps to teach balance and improves footwork.

28. WHISTLE DRILL

This drill is shown in Diagram 8-14. The drill helps to check a player's reaction for starting and stopping. All players line up at the end line. As the coach blows the whistle, the players sprint as fast as they can. When the whistle blows again, all players are to stop in position. Then the whistle blows again and the procedure is repeated. After the players touch the far end line, they run backwards to the original starting position, again stopping if a whistle sounds.

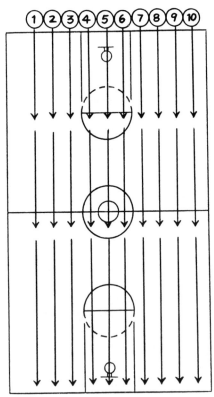

8-14

29. ZIGZAG DRILL

The zigzag drill illustrated in Diagram 8-15 is a good conditioner and also provides dribbling and footwork practice. The team is divided into groups of two according to speed. One player is on offense and the other on defense. The first pair of players start out with the defensive man putting pressure on the ball. At the first hash mark the player changes hands and dribbles for the half-court line on the opposite side of the floor. When the first pair of players get to the hash mark, the second pair begins the same routine. The first pair then goes to the hash mark on the opposite side of the floor and, finally, to the last end line in the opposite corner. The players then sprint back to their original positions where the offensive man goes on defense and vice-versa. This is repeated three times.

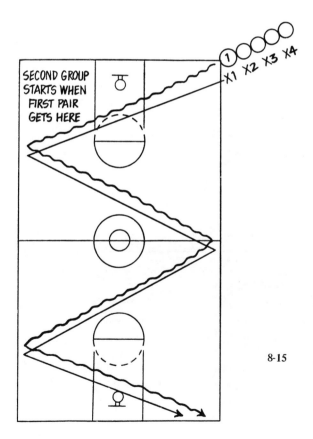

8-15

30. TWO-BALL WARM-UP DRILL

This drill is illustrated in Diagram 8-16. We use this occasionally as a pregame warm-up drill. Timing as well as passing coordination is taught.

You have two post players, A and B, in the high-post area and the remaining players are in two lines in backcourt. Player one dribbles left and then passes to post player B. Player two dribbles right and then passes to post player A. From here, they each cut through the lane with the player on the left, player one, going first. On their cuts, player one will receive the ball from post A and player two will receive his pass from post B.

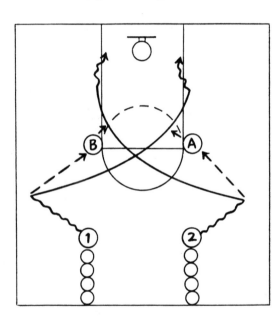

8-16

Improving Free-Throw
Percentage

Free-throw accuracy in basket-
ball has become more important each year. With today's accele-
rated game causing more fouls, the team with the good free-throw
shooters is always in the ballgame. Statistics have proved that
about one-third of all points are scored by way of the free-throw
line.

Of the many factors determining a victory or a defeat in
basketball, free-throw shooting has to rank very high. Yet many
coaches put very little or no emphasis on the free throw, and the
art of free-throw shooting has been sadly neglected at many
schools. Here is the simplest shot of all: It is truly free! When the
referee hands the player the basketball at the free-throw line, it is
the signal that no one can bother him while he aims and fires. He
is only 15 feet from the basket and it is a straightaway shot.

What makes the shot so difficult? Maybe the shooter feels the
pressure of the eyes of the crowd on him. He also has time to
think of the importance of the shot. (Maybe this shot will win or
lose the game or will put his team into the lead at this stage of the
contest.) In these few seconds, he can tighten up or worry about
missing the shot. All of a sudden the basket shrinks to the size of a
doughnut. And did you ever try to get a basketball into a
doughnut?

My advice to the player is for him to keep telling himself that this is an easy shot and that he is going to make it. He should have no doubt in his mind. He knows he is going to make it. He should "think" the ball right into the basket.

The free throw is an uncontested shot where the shooter is free to use the soundest mechanics, without the necessity of worrying about opposition. At Elgin, we place much emphasis on the importance of the charity toss and stress the following to the members of our squad:

1. The difference between winning and losing many games is the successful free throw. Over the years, we have averaged nearly nine victories per season in games in which we have been outscored from the field but still managed to win by way of the free throw.

2. A team must strive to make 70% of its free throws each game. Over the last ten years, we have averaged 72.5% from the line.

3. Because of the one-and-one rule, a good free-throw shooting team can make an average of 16-20 points per game from the line. Approximately one-third of a team's total points come from the foul line. During one season we scored 445 field goals and 493 free throws, which means that nearly 36% of our points came from the line.

4. The reliable free-throw shooters will receive more than average consideration when the coach selects a starting unit.

5. The player should realize that free-throw prowess means less contact by the opposition, more points and, possibly, a college scholarship.

Ten seconds are allowed to prepare for and execute the free throw, and the same conditions of distance and position on the court exist every time. No other shot in basketball allows the player the time or the choice of delivery that he has in the free throw. The key is practice. The more you practice, the smoother your delivery. Even a team with a poor field-goal percentage can be a good free-throw squad.

The 77% we shot as a team from the charity stripe during one season came close to the national prep record of 79.2% by Valparaiso, Indiana High School some years back. By way of comparison, the major-college record was set by Ohio State with 80.9%, while the professional standard was set years ago by the old Syracuse Nationals, 79.4%.

Through my playing experiences and coaching career I have been made a *free-throw believer!* I learned early the values of successful free-throw shooting. Years back, while playing for a Gary, Indiana team, we won the National Industrial Championship at Akron, Ohio over a New Jersey team, 88-85, by making 38 of 41 charity tosses. We made 25 field goals while our opponents made 36! Personally, I remember this game because I was fortunate to have made 22 free throws out of 22 attempts. However, I was a little embarrassed by my personal box score in the championship contest. It read 22 free throws and no baskets for a grand total of 22 points!

Free-throw shooting *can* be taught, and the coaching staff at Elgin is convinced that we put much emphasis on this phase of the game. Over a ten-year period, spanning 277 games, our teams have averaged 72.5% from the foul line and have won 89 games in which our opponents have outscored us from the field. As you can see, successful free-throw shooting not only wins games for your teams but can also turn coaching records into winners too.

At Chesterton, Indiana High School our teams averaged slightly under 70% over a five-year span. In one contest, we made 21 for 21 in a 61-58 victory. At Shabbona High School, our teams were 69.6%, 71.3% and 74.6% over a three-year period. Shabbona's team record up to that time had been 66%. At Elgin St. Edward High School our teams were 71.5% and 77%, breaking the old school mark of 63.4%. Recently, we had the added honor of capturing the Annual National Free Throw Contest sponsored by Milwaukee (Messmer) High School. This is a postal contest (conducted by mail) and we finished with a 19-1 record, just edging out defending champion Valparaiso, Indiana, who finished 18-2. Over a 15-week period, our best ten free-throw shooters canned 9,371 free throws out of a possible 10,000, while Valpo made 9,075. High schools from the following states were represented in the contest: Illinois, Indiana, Wisconsin, Michigan, New York, Ohio, Texas, California, Maryland, Iowa, Kentucky, Louisiana, Nebraska, South Carolina, Arizona, Minnesota and New Hampshire. (More about the National Free Throw Contest later in this chapter.)

The 13 St. Edward Steps to Successful
Free-Throw Shooting

1. Establish a definite routine. The player should establish the same routine in practice as he does in a game. Adopt one style as quickly as possible and stick with it. If you do something the same way enough times, a high degree of proficiency will result.
2. Dry hands and fingers before entering the free-throw circle. Shake the arms and wrists to relieve tension.
3. Take your time going to the line. This gives you a chance to catch your breath.
4. Take a stance in which you feel comfortable. Line up in the same position each time. *Relax*. Locate the exact center of the free-throw line. (We have the floor marked for the exact center.) Place the toe of the right foot (if you are righthanded) exactly on the marked spot pointing towards the basket. Place the toe of the left foot parallel to the right foot, about 1-5 inches behind the line.
5. Bounce the ball a few times to get the feel of it. You can wiggle the ball a few times if that also helps give you the feel of the ball.
6. Assume the starting shooting position. Locate the needle hole and place your second finger on top of this valve, which serves as a centering point for the shooter. The ball is held just below eye level and about 10-12 inches in front of the right eye. Also, placing the finger on the valve insures holding the ball the same way each time. It also places the hand behind the ball and not on the side of it.
7. Take one or two deep breaths; this helps calm the body. Grip the ball firmly, yet softly. Hold the ball on the third phalanges of the fingers, not on the palm. Place the non-shooting hand on the side of the ball.
8. Sight the basket and concentrate. Think positively. Aim for the target just over the near rim of the basket. This ball is a small object and the basket is a large target.
9. The ball is brought down and toward the chin to begin the shot. The knees are slightly flexed.

10. Think about keeping the ball as straight as possible. Keep the head as still as possible. This is for proper balance.

11. Let the ball roll off your fingertips and give a good wrist snap.

12. Make a complete follow through (See Photo 9-1). Throw with smoothness and rhythm. A continuous motion is a necessity. When releasing the ball, cock the wrist with the thumb touching the second and third fingers. Bring the hand forward and downward for good follow through. A good follow through forces the shot to be soft. As the arc is completed, the knees, ankles, arm and wrist are extended completely for the follow through.

13. Always notice where the ball lands. If you miss you will be able to make adjustments.

Photo 9-1

If a player can make 70% of his shots from the foul line, we leave him alone to use any style he wishes. We do not try to alter his style unless the player asks for advice.

We advocate the one-hand set shot for free throwing. This type free throw seems to correspond closely to that of the jump shot or set shot. However, if the player can consistently shoot 70% or above with another method, such as the underhanded, two-hand overhead, or jumpshot free throw, he may shoot his own way.

Eleven Common Free-Throw Faults

1. Failure to concentrate on the basket. You should look at the near edge of the rim and hit the hole right over the rim. Too often, a player will watch the ball in flight.
2. Failure to locate the exact center of the foul line. The feet should be placed in relation to this mark on every shot.
3. Failure to shoot off the fingertips. Shooting off the palm results in a "flat" attempt.
4. Failure to follow through in direct line with the basket. The shooting hand should come up directly between the eyes. Jerking the hands off the ball or stopping motion at the point of release will cause a faulty shot.
5. Failure to balance by rocking backward on the rear foot. Also, the improper shifting of body weight from the back to the front during the shot.
6. Failure to have the knees bent properly. The knees should bend slightly.
7. Failure to have the proper arc. Medium arc is best. Too often, the ball has too much arc or a "flat" arc.
8. Failure to have proper elbow movement. Sometimes the elbow of the shooter is out to the side instead of in front of the shoulder.
9. Failure to have proper hand placement. Sometimes the player will have the free hand too far around in front of the ball, instead of on the side.
10. Failure to keep the head as still as possible.
11. Failure to drop the ball to chin level. In younger players,

especially, there is a bad habit of dropping the ball to any place between the waist and chest prior to the shot.

Our Favorite Drills and Gimmicks

The following drills and gimmicks have been tested and proved successful for us over several years. Each drill is designed to bring about a certain amount of game-like pressure on the player.

There is nothing more frustrating in basketball than to outshoot the opponents from the field and yet lose the game on the foul line. The answer to better free-throw shooting is practice—not just freely shooting the ball, but pressure-simulated work. Thanks to an organized plan of attack, we have been able to win 89 games in which we have been outscored from the field by our opponents. In one game our opponents made 31 field goals to our 19 but we won the game by making 33 of 39 free throws. Our opponents made 6 of 19 from the line in our 71-68 victory.

We stress and incorporate the following points in our free-throw program:

1. A variety of drills and not monotony.
2. Fun while learning.
3. Practice helps build confidence.
4. Make the practice situation as game-like as possible.

1. MORNING FREE THROWS

The players come in one-half hour before school begins (in our case at 7:30 a.m.) and we have orange juice and doughnuts for them. Each boy shoots 20 free throws and has to make 16 to get his juice and doughnuts. The tab (15c) is picked up by the coaching staff. If the boy is unsuccessful in making at least 16 shots, he pays the 15c bill. Needless to say, after January, the coaching staff goes broke fast! In late February, we require 17 of 20.

2. LADDER BOARD

Any player either one or two steps below another player on the "ladder" offers the challenge (See Diagram 9-1). Each player must accept at least one challenge each day. Each player shoots 15 free throws in groups of five. No challenge can be made more than 24 hours in advance. The winner trades steps with the loser if he was below him on the ladder. A malt or shake is awarded to the winner on the first day of each month.

NOTE: As a variation, we go in order each day such as one plays two, three plays four, etc., with the losers dropping each day to the bottom of the ladder and the winners moving up a notch.

9-1

ST. EDWARD FREE THROW LADDER BOARD

- CHRIS DOLAN
- DENNY BUTZOW
- CRAIG HEDLEY
- JEFF NOLAN
- BOB SAUCEDA
- R. ALTERS
- JOE PALUMBO
- TERRY WAHL
- STEVE PAVLIK
- NORM HANSEN
- DAVE BELL
- MARK WHALEN
- BOB HARNEY

3. CONSECUTIVE 75 CLUB

We do this drill about 20-25 times a year. We have each player pair off with a partner and shoot for a consecutive number of free throws made. When he misses, his partner starts a string, and vice-versa. If a boy makes over 75 consecutive free throws, he becomes a lifetime member of the 75 Club and receives a patch for his letter jacket. We have had eight boys make the club, with the high totals being 98 by Rod Fultz and 92 by Chris Dolan. Fultz made over 75 on nine occasions and Dolan made over 75 four times.

4. PRACTICE FREE-THROW GRAPHS (See Diagram 9-2)

Each player is allowed to shoot free throws until he misses three. On the graph, a mark is made by the number the player made before missing the third shot. For example, if the player shoots 15 free throws and the 15th shot is miss number three, you would mark 12 on the graph. The players normally pair off for this drill.

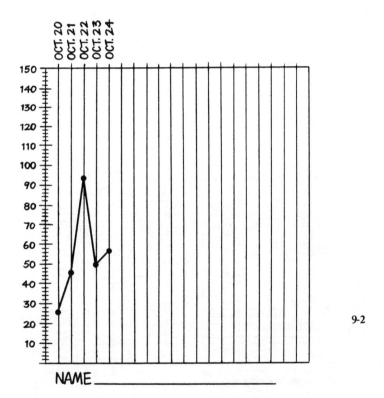

9-2

5. TEAM FREE-THROW GRAPH (See Diagram 9-3)

This graph is made before the first ballgame of the season. The names of the opposing teams are inserted vertically in the space on top. The number of free throws attempted in each game and the number made are shown. At the close of each game, the percentage is marked at the bottom. The next game the same procedure is followed. A line is drawn from the first mark to the second mark, etc., throughout the season. At the close of the season, you have an accurate check on free-throw shooting in the games for the entire season.

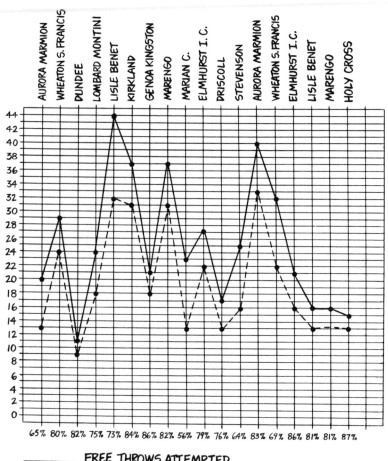

9-3

6. POSTAL CONTEST BETWEEN INDIVIDUAL SCHOOLS
(See Diagram 9-4)

This is a team and individual contest conducted by mail with another school. Each game, the coach lists his top five free-throw shooters in that contest. If a situation exists where only three of four players shoot free throws in a game, the fourth and fifth players have to be listed as zero per cent. Point distribution is two points for each individual player with the highest percentage and a bonus of three points for the team with the highest percentage for that game. In case of a tie on percentages, the player with the most free throws made that game is the winner. If both players make the same number of free throws and the same percentage, one point is awarded to each player. A running total of points is kept after each game. The total possible points each game is 13 points: 10 individual and 3 bonus for team. At the end of the season, the top five players (with at least 40 attempts) for each team are matched against each other with two points awarded to each player. A bonus of ten points is given to the team (all players) with the highest percentage. This total is added to the running total determining the grand winner. We have had individual contests with Shabbona, Illinois High School and Milwaukee (Messmer) High School.

7. NATIONAL FREE-THROW CONTEST (See Diagram 9-5)

This is an annual free-throw contest sponsored by Milwaukee (Messmer) High School of Wisconsin. This is also a mail contest. We were fortunate to win a recent contest and become National Free-Throw Champions. Our players actually looked forward each week to the new out-of-state opponent as one week it would be Pensacola, Florida, the next week Eden Prairie, Minnesota, etc. Rules of the contest state that, each week, ten free-throw shooters from one team, rated in order of the best through worst, 1-10, competed against the ten rated marksmen from another school. Each player attempted 50 shots and the player making the most was awarded two points. The total score wins, plus a bonus of

TEAM <u>ELGIN ST. EDWARD</u>   GAME <u>#25</u>   TEAM <u>SHABBONA</u>

	GAME	PCT.	PTS.			GAME	PCT.	PTS.
HEDLEY	6-6	1,000	0	FULTZ		9-9	1,000	2
BUTZOW	2-2	1,000	0	SCHOU		5-5	1,000	2
SAUCEDA	1-1	1,000	2	ESPE		5-6	83	0
DOLAN	7-8	88	2	OLESON		4-6	67	0
ALTERS	5-8	63	2	CRAIG		1-4	25	0

TOTAL PCT. THIS GAME <u>78</u>   TOTAL PCT. THIS GAME <u>80</u>
TOTAL PTS. THIS GAME ——— <u>6</u>   TOTAL PTS. THIS GAME ——— <u>7</u>

RUNNING TOTAL POINTS SEASON <u>ELGIN</u>   166   <u>SHABBONA</u>   159

FINAL SEASON STATISTICS

	SEASON	PCT.	PTS.			SEASON	PCT.	PTS.
DOLAN	112-137	82	0	FULTZ		140-161	87	2
ALTERS	77-101	77	0	OLESON		81-105	77	2
HEDLEY	81-105	77	2	SCHOU		52-68	76	0
NOLAN	82-114	72	2	MILLER		43-67	64	0
SAUCEDA	49-71	71	2	ESPE		54-91	59	0

SEASON PCT. <u>76.5</u>   SEASON PCT. <u>71.3</u>
TOTAL PTS. <u>16</u>   TOTAL PTS. <u>4</u>

FINAL SCORE: <u>ELGIN ST. EDWARD</u>   182
               <u>SHABBONA</u>   163

9-4

three points for the team making the most free throws, thus giving a school a possible 23 points in a given match. Tie matches count as one-half the total points. League standings are kept and sent periodically as are the total free throws. Our record in 1972 was 19-1 and we made 9,371 out of a possible 10,000 free throws. (Any school desiring information on entering the contest should contact Dave (Dusty) Rhodes at Messmer High School, Milwaukee, Wisconsin.)

8. CHOKE OUT (See Diagram 9-6)

Players line up in single file at the free-throw line. When a

NATIONAL FREE THROW CONTEST

WEEK OF JANUARY 22, 1972

ELGIN ST. EDWARD	VS	MILWAUKEE MESSMER

TEAM RECORD __16-0__   TEAM RECORD __14-2__
COACH __BOB FULLER__   COACH __DUSTY RHODES__

	MADE OUT OF 50	PTS.		MADE OUT OF 50	PTS.
DOLAN	47	2	McGREGOR	44	0
BUTZOW	46	2	VIGO	44	0
NOLAN	43	0	KMIEPPEL	48	2
HEDLEY	42	0	HECHT	43	2
ALTERS	43	1	CHERUBINI	43	1
SAUCEDA	44	1	MATOUSHEK	44	1
HANSEN	43	2	SCHRAMKA	38	0
PAULIK	41	0	DUPRIES	45	2
WAHL	43	2	SEEFELDT	38	0
PALUMBO	40	0	VOLLY	41	2

TOTAL TEAM __432__   TOTAL TEAM __428__

FINAL SCORE: __ELGIN__   13   __MILWAUKEE__   10

NEXT GAME: __BATTLE CREEK, MICHIGAN__

9-5

player makes a shot, the player directly behind him must make the shot, or he chokes out and must make 25 free throws on the side basket. If the first two men in line miss and the third player makes the free throw, then the number-two player is out. This is continued until a champion is declared.

9. END-OF-PRACTICE DRILL

We run this drill in two variations. In the number-one phase, each boy has to make ten in a row before going home. In the number-two phase, the entire team lines up and each player has to make a free throw. For example, if you have 12 players, the team would have to make 12 in a row before heading to the showers.

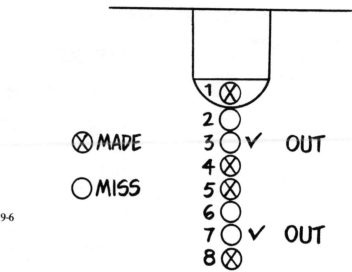

⊗ MADE

◯ MISS

9-6

10. TEN FREE THROWS OR RUN

When a player first steps on the court for practice, he takes no other shot but a free throw for his first ten attempts. The boy shoots ten and the number he misses represents the number of laps he will run.

11. CONSECUTIVE SWISHERS

The players are divided into groups of two. Each boy shoots a maximum of five free throws and his partner rebounds. The object of the drill is to see how many combined consecutive free throws can be made. The catch is, the ball cannot touch anything but the net. If the ball touches any part of the rim it counts as a miss.

12. ONE-AND-ONE OR RUN

The players divide up with four to a basket. The first player shoots one shot and, if he misses, he runs two laps and returns to his group at the end of his line. If he misses the second shot he runs only one lap. If he makes both free throws he does not run but returns to the end of his line.

13. CONSECUTIVE TEN-MINUTE DRILL

Divide your squad into two teams. Put ten minutes on the scoreboard clock. Each player at each end of the court shoots two free throws at a time. Only the consecutive team total is kept. Whenever a player misses, the consecutive free throws at the time of the miss represents how many laps he is to run. For example, if the team has 12 in a row, the player who misses must run 12 laps. At the end of the ten-minute time period the team with the high consecutive total is the winner and the losers have a penalty to run.

14. YOU'RE IT—INDIVIDUAL BONUS DRILL

This is another drill that can be used at the end of practice or interspersed throughout a practice. The squad lines up at the end line and runs a set of lines (See Chapter 1). The coach selects one player to shoot a one-on-one free throw. If he makes both free throws, the practice or the drill is over. If he misses either of the tosses, the entire squad runs another set of lines. At the end of this run the squad selects the shooter and the same rules apply again.

15. 80% DRILL

Here is another drill that can be used effectively at the end of practice. The entire team lines up single file at the free-throw stripe. Each player has two free throws and the entire team must make 80% of their tosses before going to the shower. For example, if you have ten players, the team would have to make at least 16 of 20.

16. 15-IN-A-ROW DRILL

We put five players at each basket. Each player has to make three free throws in a row before moving on to the next drill. For example, using five boys, the team total would be 15 consecutive free throws.

17. BLINDFOLD SHOOTING

If a muscular pattern and rhythm has been developed, the player can shoot a free throw with surprising ability. We have the players pair off and each player makes the best of ten. We have the players shoot with a blindfold placed over the eyes. The eyes must be kept open for balance. We have had boys make 7 of 10.

18. CLOSED-EYES DRILLS

This is very similar to the blindfold drill and an excellent drill for getting the feel of the free throw. After going through the procedure of getting ready for the shot, close your eyes while shooting. You will find that players who have perfected this technique will be able to make 8 out of 10.

19. TEAM BONUS FREE-THROW DRILL

Team A and Team B play three rounds. Each player shoots a one-and-bonus free throw. If he misses the first shot, he does not get the bonus. If you have two teams of five players, the perfect score for one team is 30. As a variation, you can divide the teams up, such as four groups of three players each, and have a four team "tournament." After the three rounds, the two winners play for the championship and the two losers play for third place.

20. FREE-THROW GAME "21" (See Diagram 9-7)

This is a three-on-three game. Players A, B and C play players one, two and three. If A makes his shot, he keeps shooting until he makes four consecutive shots. At that time, his teammates B or C will shoot. Any time he misses, a teammate becomes the shooter until all members of one team have had a turn. Then one, two and three take turns shooting. When a shooter misses, his teammates try for an offensive rebound score. If the defense rebounds it stops the play action. Each basket scores two points and each free throw one point. The game is "21."

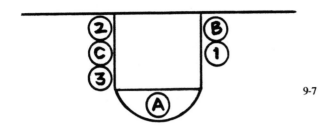

9-7

21. WORST-SHOOTER DRILL

Divide the squad into groups of two. One group challenges another group. Each player in each group shoots 15 shots, a total of 30 for a team. The winning group goes to the showers while the losing group has to stay and challenge another losing group. In this round, each player shoots ten, with a team total of 20. The next round for the losing teams will be five each and a team total of ten. Finally, the last two players on the same team shoot the best of ten. The loser shoots 25 after everybody has showered and also earns the worst free-throw shooter award.

22. INDIVIDUAL MINI-TOURNAMENT

We have the players get into groups of two. Each player shoots five free throws with the winner being declared on the best of five. In case of a tie, the player who shoots last shoots a sudden-death shot. If he makes it he is the winner and if he misses his opponent is the winner. The winners rotate clockwise with the losers staying home and shooting last for the sudden-death advantage. We have a portable blackboard put in the middle of the floor with the players names and a wins-and-losses column. The winners record their wins and the opponents' losses before rotating to the next basket.

23. INDIVIDUAL FREE-THROW GRAPH

The players' game-by-game percentages are recorded in the same way as the Team Graph, as detailed in Diagram 9-2.

24. "25"

Players are in groups of two. The first player to make a free throw gets one point. The same player continues to shoot from the foul line scoring two points for each shot. He shoots until he misses. When there is a miss, the opponent gets the ball. The player scoring 25 points first is the winner and the loser has a penalty.

25. STOP-PRACTICE DRILL

We often stop practice at seven or eight intervals and have a different player at each interval shoot two free throws. For each shot the player misses, the entire team has to do a lap or a line after practice.

26. GIMMICK TO CHECK PROPER BALL RELEASE

We have the free-throw shooting player grip the ball so that a taped or painted stripe is between the index and middle fingers. If the ball is released properly, the stripe will not wobble but will give the appearance of a straight line.

27. FREE-THROW SHOOTER OF THE WEEK (See Diagram 9-8)

Our manager records the number made out of 50 free throws per day for each player. At the end of the week, the player with the highest total is awarded a pair of sweat socks. Also, a monthly running total is kept and, at the end of the season, an award is given to the Free-Throw Shooter of the Year.

FREE THROW SHOOTER OF THE WEEK
DEC. 6-12 WEEK

	MON.	TUES.	WED.	THURS.	FRI.	SAT.	TOTAL	TOTAL FOR YEAR	(7 WKS.)
CHRIS DOLAN	48	45	44	46		49	232	1347	
CRAIG HEDLEY	42	42	43	50		42	219	1302	
JEFF NOLAN	39	46	41	45		43	214	1313	
BOB SAUCEDA	45	38	41	44		39	207	1302	

9-8

28. SMALL-RINGS GIMMICK

We attach small rings to the inside of our baskets on special days. These rings allow the ball to go through the ring freely but they require a higher degree of skill than do the regular goals.

29. TWO-MINUTE DRILL

The squad is divided into groups of two. The number of consecutive free throws made for the team determines the winner. There is a two-minute time limit. The maximum free throws at one time for each boy is five.

30. DAYS OF THE GAME

We always shoot free throws on days when we have games. For example, if we have a Friday night game, we usually come in after school for 20 minutes to shoot free throws in our tennis shoes and regular school clothes. If we play Saturday night, we usually shoot around 11:00 a.m.

Our main formula to free throw success is, again, *practice*. There will be many days, especially in the early season, when our ballplayers will shoot as many as 200 or more free throws a day. If a player is able to practice a particular skill this many times, some improvement in skill will be achieved.

10.

Improving Field-Goal
Percentage

Not too many years ago, most coaches had their players all shooting one way, according to a clear-cut style delineated by the coach. At Elgin St. Edward High School, we allow the boys to use their own styles. It makes sense. Our kids begin shooting (usually) at a early age and, by the time they reach high school, some of them have a style of their own. The only boy we tamper with is the boy who continually shows a bad percentage or is making an obvious mistake that has to be corrected.

Shooters are made and *not* born. It is true that some players do possess more "natural" talent than others. An important point to remember is that you cannot become a shooter during the season; it must be done in the off-season with hours and hours of practice. Satisfactory shooting can be taught.

Most players like to shoot and will spend hours perfecting their favorite shot. No other aspect of our great game of "roundball" has developed to such a degree of common skill as shooting. Shooting percentages improve each winter. It is not uncommon for a high school team to shoot 46-50 per cent from the field for a complete game. The time will come when any shooting percentage less than 50% will prove ineffective.

Over a ten-year period spanning 277 games, our teams have a

composite 45% field-goal average. Over the last five campaigns, our teams have shot 42.6%, 45%, 48.3% 43.7% and 46%.

In 37 of these games, we shot over 60% from the field. In one game, we shot 69.2%, winning the game 53-50; and in another game, we shot 69.6% in a 76-39 win. I feel that the 45% accuracy figure is even more impressive when it is considered that we do not usually get our share of layup or short-shot attempts because of our size limitations over the years.

We stress field-goal shooting in practice and much emphasis is put on this phase of the game. It is proved over and over again that teams with high field-goal percentages are strong contenders and consistent winners.

Using analogies for field-goal shooting as we did for free-throw shooting in the last chapter, we find that the highest field-goal percentage ever recorded by a major college team is 54.4% by Ohio State. For the professionals, the highest team record is 48.8% by the Milwaukee Bucks. The one-game field-goal percentage mark for a major college team was set by Minnesota, 72.3 (versus Iowa) back in 1960.

It is possible for the weakest, smallest boy on a team to develop into a good shooter. It may be impossible for him to be a good rebounder. Most players are eager to improve their accuracy and will cooperate fully with the coach. It is the coach's job to drill his players over and over in the correct shooting techniques until they become automatic. Proper technique is the answer to shooting. This means practicing the precise fundamentals so that these become second nature.

We can teach the boy how to hold the ball, how to position his arm as he shoots, how to flex his wrist before he shoots. We always demonstrate at one of our first meetings how easy shooting can be, by standing on a ladder and dropping two basketballs side by side through the basket at the same time. (Two basketballs side by side will actually fit in the basket.) Encourage the boys to think of the little ball and the big basket (See Photo 10-1).

I would like to point out one pertinent fact before going into the various techniques of each shot. If a boy, no matter how poor his shooting form is, can consistently shoot well, we will not tamper with him. For example, if a boy can consistently score on his jump shot by fading sideways instead of going straight up and

Photo 10-1

down, he can continue fading sideways. We learned this lesson early. In my first year of coaching we "discovered" a boy who had been shooting consistently (around 45%) with a flaw in his form. He was shooting the ball off the palms of his hand. We worked hours and hours getting the boy to shoot the ball off his fingertips. The result was the boy shooting in the low 30% range, until we allowed the boy to go back to his original "style" and, immediately, his percentage climbed.

Steps to Improve Field-Goal Accuracy

We use the following steps or "tips" to help teach shooting:
1. Explain and demonstrate the fundamentals.
2. Require all boys to shoot only when they are under control and on balance.
3. Provide as many basketballs as possible, because the more balls that are available, the more shooting opportunities the team will have.
4. Start a shot from one position, close to the basket, and don't worry about violations such as traveling, etc.

5. Shoot the shot from this position at least 20 times. Through repetition, the muscles form a groove.
6. Have drills to make players shoot from all spots on the floor. Spot shooters are too easily defended. Teach players several floor shots.
7. Practice one part of the shot at a time. Work on the eyes; work on the wrist; work on the follow through. Don't try to do everything at once.
8. Have the player work on eliminating shooting habits that give an advantage to an opponent, for example, a player who has to bounce the ball once before shooting. A good defensive man is quick to pick up this flaw.
9. As you progress and can hit the shot, make the moves into the shot. Dribble on both sides of the court and shoot. Practice receiving a pass and then shooting.
10. Play shooting games such as horse, "21" and other games (Described later in this chapter).
11. Play one on one basketball and practice the shots you don't make very often, such as jump shots going left, etc.
12. All shooting practice must be supervised by the coaching staff in order to prevent the development of incorrect shooting habits.
13. Practice . . . practice . . . practice. This helps to develop poise, confidence and concentration.

There are many different shots in today's game. Among them are: the one-hand layup shot; two-hand overhead shot (layup); twisting layup shot; running one-hand shot; one-hand set shot; two-hand overheld set shot; two-handed set shot; two-handed overhead jumpshot; one-hand jumpshot; tip-in shot; turnaround shot; hook shot; two-hand underhand sweepshot.

This chapter will deal with the shots we stress in our program, namely, the one-hand layup, one-hand set, one-hand jump shot and hookshot.

The fundamentals taught by our coaching staff in developing the layup are listed below. The shooter is on the right side of the basket shooting with his right hand. If the shooter is on the left side, substitute the word left for right, and vice-versa.

The Layup Shot

1. The layup is a very difficult shot to master. The righthanded shooter should plant his left foot and bring his right leg up high to allow maximum extension of the right arm in releasing the ball.
2. The shooter should look up, focus his eyes at a point on the backboard above and to the right of the goal.
3. At the peak of the shooter's jump, he stretches still higher by raising the right shoulder. When the right shoulder and arm are fully extended, the ball is softly shot by the right hand and wrist.
4. After being removed from the ball, the left hand and arm offer some protection from the opponent.
5. The shot should be a high jump, not a broad jump. The shooter should land almost directly under the basket.
6. Most of the force applied in making the shot comes from the fingers and wrist. The ball should be put up softly.

The reverse layup is approached from the opposite side of the basket from which the shot is made. The takeoff is from the foot opposite the strong hand. With the head slightly backward to see the target point on the backboard, the ball is carried upward with both hands. At full extension, the off hand falls away and the shooting hand releases the ball backward off the backboard.

Concerning the one-hand layup shot, coaches still do not agree on the method of shooting this shot. One theory is that the hand should be behind the ball and the palm facing the backboard. Another theory is that the ball should be released with the hand underneath the ball, allowing it to roll off the fingers. At Elgin, we stress the former method, but both seem acceptable. The choice seems many times to depend upon the angle and position of the shooter. We do not change a boy's style unless he is having trouble; then we will tell him which method to use.

Some common errors in shooting the layup are jumping off the wrong foot, laying the ball off the backboard too hard and broad jumping. This may seem, to some coaches, to be too elementary a shot to emphasize strongly. These coaches say that the layup shot is taught in the early grades and that the high-school coach shouldn't have to stress it. I can well remember my first year at Elgin and working with a senior player, who had nine years of basketball experience behind him, and yet could not shoot a layup properly. We worked many hours on him just to get him to take off from the proper foot. My point is that nothing in basketball should be taken for granted.

The Jump Shot (Photos 10-2 and 10-3)

The jump shot is one of the most effective offensive weapons in the Wishbone Offense. A fast, accurate jump shot is virtually impossible to stop.

1. Go up on the balls of both feet simultaneously. One foot should not be in front of the other, but the feet should be even with one another. You can jump a lot higher when your feet are even. If one foot is in front of the other, the force is not going up through the hips and the shoulders. As a gimmick, have the boy try jumping with one foot in front of the other. Then have the boy jump with the feet even. You will no doubt find that he can jump higher when the feet are even.

2. On the jump, go straight up and come down on the spot from which you started. As a gimmick, we use a hula hoop or place a circle made of tape on the floor at different shot ranges and have the players go up and come down inside the circle.

3. Grip the ball firmly yet softly with the right hand (for righthanders) in the center of the ball, the middle finger serving as a fulcrum point. Put the left hand on the left side of the ball. Fingers of both hands should be spread. The palm of neither hand should touch the ball; shoot the ball from your fingertips.

   The hands should be held just below the waist as the jump shot starts. Don't hold the hands too high because you won't be able to get enough spring in your jump to get into the air. As a gimmick, have the boy stand under the basket without the ball and jump as high as he can and touch the backboard. You'll probably notice two things:

Photo 10-2

one, that the boy's feet will probably be even when he starts his jump; and two, he'll drop his hands down by his knees as he starts his jump. The same should be true on the jump shot. Now have the boy jump up and touch the backboard with his hands even with his shoulders. Don't let him lower his hands as he tries to jump. Notice the difference. So have your hands drop below your waist with your hands on the side of the ball, not on the top.

4. Keep your eyes on the target—the entire target. Concentrate on putting the ball just over the near edge of the rim. Do not watch the ball in flight. Keep your eyes on the basket until the ball goes through the net.

5. Ball position should be in front of and above the head so

Photo 10-3

that the shooter may sight just above the ball. Do not let
the ball go too far back on your head because if it does,
you'll have to throw the ball to get it to the basket. Do not
get the ball too high off your forehead. When this happens
the arm straightens out. With the arm straight, you lose
some of the power necessary to propel the ball up to the
basket. Remember, you'll get more power, you'll have a
softer shot and one that is easier to control if you'll place
the ball above the forehead on the shot.

6. Release the ball at the peak of the jump. Simply let the
   legs start the shot and, as soon as they do, jerk your arms
   up to the top of your forehead. This will give you the

maximum jumping power. As a gimmick, we sometimes use a screen that can be adjusted to different heights. Since the boy cannot see the basket until he gets above the screen, this gimmick will also sharpen his reactions in picking up the target.

7. When at the peak of the jump, release the ball with as little backspin as possible imparted to the ball by wrist action. When releasing the ball, cock the wrist with the thumb touching the second and third fingers. The elbow and wrist are probably the two most important parts of any jump shot. The wrist, when the ball is just off the forehead and is about to be shot, should be bent as much as possible. This supplies the power and the soft touch to the shot. If the wrist is not bent, you have very little control over the shot. As you look at your wrists when you are shooting, there should be wrinkles in it, and that means it is bent as much as possible. As a gimmick, place the boy on the left side of the basket at a range of about three feet. Have the boy square himself with the backboard, extend his forearm, check for proper grip, and bank the ball into the basket using wrist and finger action. The position automatically enforces good form.

8. A snap of the wrist releases the ball toward its target. The shoulders should be square with the basket at the instant of release. The arms should not throw the ball; the wrist must be used. The ball should roll off the fingertips, which gives backspin to insure true flight. You can increase your wrist power by such simple exercises as squeezing a small rubber ball in your hands, doing pushups, wall pushaways and working with light weights (5 to 10 lbs.). As a gimmick, if a boy is using his left hand to push the ball, we tape his thumb to his index finger.

9. After shooting, bring the hand forward and downward to establish good follow through. If correct action is used, the shooter will land on balance. As a gimmick to check release, we have the boy grip the ball so that a painted or taped stripe on the ball is between his index and middle fingers. If the ball is released properly, the stripe will not wobble but will give the appearance of a straight line.

10. On the follow through, your body should be coming down in about the same position it was in when it went up into the air. Don't jump too far forward and definitely don't jump to the side. As you shoot, the hand and arm should be toward the basket on the follow through and the elbow should be relatively straight. If you are following through correctly, the ball should have a spin as it goes through the basket. This spin is extremely important because it leads to a soft shot.

11. All concentration and thought during the shot should be on the target. The shooter can even follow through mentally to make sure he is concentrating fully. Think the ball into the basket.

12. Shoot a "dead" ball. Handle the ball as if it were an egg that should break if it were handled roughly. Shoot the ball instead of guiding it.

The Hook Shot (Photo 10-4)

This is a very effective shot that requires long, hard hours of practice to develop. It is also a hard shot to teach. We use the hook shot quite extensively in our baseline-series options. The following are the actions of a righthanded shooter on the right side of the floor. The glaring advantage of the hook shoot is that the ball is released from a spot at which it is difficult to block. The player has his left arm and his whole body between the ball and his defensive man.

1. (Back to the basket), the righthanded shooter makes his first step with the left foot at an angle that keeps him away from the defensive man but not from the basket. The shooter is on the right side of the goal.

2. He turns his head and looks at the basket.

3. The toe of the lead foot should never point away from the basket.

4. When the shooter completes his shot, he should be facing the basket ready to go in either direction to get the ball.

5. The right arm is straightened fully just before the ball is released. The left arm acts as a protective barrier against the

defensive man. This is often called the stiff-arm shot.

6. The left leg is fully extended and may leave the floor briefly. The right leg is lifted with the shot.

Photo 10-4

The One-Hand Set Shot

This shot is most effective 15 to 25 feet from the basket. I feel that the one-hand set is the most generally successful and reliable shot available at long range, if the player is given enough time to make it.

Even though we stress the one-hand set shot only sparingly, I will include it in this section for two reasons: one, it was the only shot I could make consistently at A.A.U. circles (it also added about six more years to my active playing career); two, I definitely feel that there is a place in every team's offense for the set shot. When perfected, the set shot has a great deal more range and accuracy than does the jump shot.

Rod Fultz, who played for me at Shabbona High School, was the best set shooter I have ever seen. Rod broke every available scoring record, averaging 47% from the field and 85% from the foul line in his three-year varsity career. This average becomes more phenomenal when you realize over 75% of Rod's baskets were scored over 18 feet from the basket! In the semi-finals of a conference tourney against Newark High School, Fultz put on the greatest one-man outside shooting exhibition it has been my pleasure ever to witness. Fultz made 16 field goals, with each goal coming from between 20 and 30 feet from the basket. We needed each goal as we nipped Newark 56 to 55 in a triple overtime. In another game that season, Fultz put on a shooting show up in Elgin, making 22 of 34 field-goal attempts and ten free throws for 54 points in our 101-70 victory.

Rod spoiled the old adage that a good shooter has to have keen eyes. Fultz, who without his glasses would be unable to play, had very poor eyes. We always kept an extra pair of glasses on the bench in case his regular pair were broken. Fultz appeared at clinics with me and never failed to amaze those in attendance with his uncanny shooting ability.

1. The position of the feet is a matter of personal choice, although many players prefer the foot under the shooting hand to be slightly forward.
2. The hand grip on the ball is the same as for the jump shot: right hand spread and palm off the ball. The left hand supports the ball on the bottom left.
3. The ball is held at chest level. The higher the ball is carried in the set position the quicker the shooter can get the ball away. The shot begins with a moderate knee dip. The ball is dropped to about chin level.
4. The position of the shooting hand is on the low back side of the ball, with the fingers spread.

5. The function of the off hand is to provide balance. The off hand falls away the instant before releasing.
6. As the shooter rises to his toes and thrusts with his legs, he simultaneously thrusts his shooting arm to full extension.
7. The shooter's hand and fingers flex downward smoothly at the wrist as the ball is released.
8. The arm should be straightened fully in the follow through with the wrist flexed downward.
9. Come back down on the balls of your feet so that you are well-balanced and ready to move quickly on the next play.

Layup-Shooting Drills

The following are our favorite layup drills, which we use frequently during the season:

1. GREEN-WAVE LAYUP DRILL

We often use this drill as a pregame warm-up routine. The players pair off, each group with a ball. The groups then play follow the leader, with one player shooting from each group and then the partners following the same type shot. We have the shooters' partners give pressure to the shooter on the layup attempt, such as a slight bump or push to simulate game conditions. The shots we use are right-hand layup, left-hand layup, right reverse, left reverse, short bank shot left, short bank shot right, and a "spinner" (a semi-hook) from the left and a spinner from the right.

The players then go into the jump-shot phase, with one player shooting and his partner rebounding from another line. The players shoot from each corner, both wing and the point.

2. DEFENSIVE-SPLIT LAYUP DRILL

The defensive-split layup drill is shown in Diagram 10-1. Defensive players X1 and X2 allow player one to get a step on them and then chase and harass the shooter, trying to cause him to miss. This is an excellent drill for teaching the player to shoot under pressure.

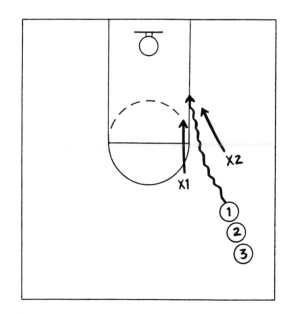

10-1

3. TEAM LAYUP DRILL

The team divides into two groups and one group goes to each end line. On a signal from the coach, the first player from each line dribbles the full length of the court for the layup basket. As soon as he scores, he passes back to the second man in line. The second man cannot leave the starting line until the ball touches his hands.

The game is "20" with each layup counting one point. Each line should yell out its actual count as this makes the game more interesting and puts a little more pressure on the shooters.

Jump-Shot and Set-Shot Drills

1. SCOREBOARD SHOOTING

The team divides into groups of two. We use the scoreboard clock and set it at eight minutes. One boy shoots continuously for one minute, with his partner rebounding, at distances of 18 to 21 feet. The shooter counts only the shots he makes.

As the end of one minute, the clock is stopped and the players exchange positions. The players alternate until the clock reads zero, with each boy having four minutes of shooting. Our managers record the players' totals at each minute interval. A good shooter should make 40 to 45 goals during his allotted shooting time. An excellent shooter will average 48-55. We make a record of the scores daily so that the boys can see an accurate evaluation of their program.

2. FOLLOW THE SHOT

The team divides into groups of two with the lines of players opposite each other in the corners of the court, facing the basket.

The player in the line on the right takes a jump shot and, as he releases the ball, the player from the opposite line runs to get the rebound along with the shooter. Both players must get to the ball before it can touch the floor. Then each player makes a layup.

If either of the players allows the ball to touch the floor, both players have ten fingertip pushups to perfrom and then they return to the drill. After this drill is completed, the players go to wing and corner positions and finally to the point and corner with all players exchanging positions.

3. COMPETITIVE-SHOOTING DRILL

The teams divide into two groups. Both teams face each other at opposite end lines. On a signal from the coach, the first player in each line dribbles to the opposite free-throw circle at full speed and shoots a shot at the key area. This drill teaches the player to shoot after going at full speed. The game is 21, with each basket counting one point.

4. HOOP SHOOTING DRILL

We place two hula hoops or tape a circle as shown in Diagram 10-2. The team is divided into groups of two. One player rebounds while the other player shoots. The shooter must shoot from a different circle each time and the drill is timed on the scoreboard for two minutes. After two minutes, the players alternate positions. A good score would be 25 in two minutes.

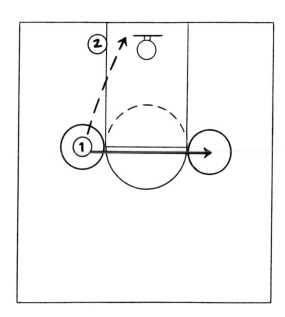

10-2

Hook-Shooting Drills

1. BASELINE-SERIES DRILL

We use the baseline series options from our Wishbone Offense as described in Chapter 2. We usually go three-on-three as shown in Diagram 2-15.

2. ROTATION DRILL

The rotation drill is illustrated in Diagram 10-3. Player one has the ball. He passes to player two, who passes to player three. Player one breaks into the lane area where he receives a pass for his hook from player three. Player one rebounds and passes to player two, who has moved to one's spot. Player one falls in behind player six.

3. TWO-LINES HOOK DRILL

The two-lines hook drill is depicted in Diagram 10-4. Player one

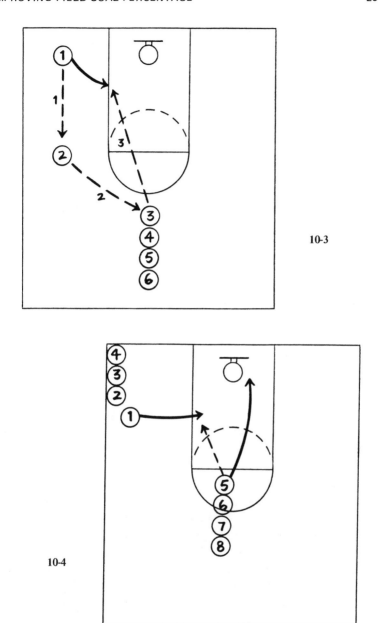

10-3

10-4

receives a pass from player five while on the move and shoots a right-hand hook shot. Player five rebounds and passes to player six, who passes to player two. All players exchange lines.

We also use the following combination drills, which are known to all basketball players and coaches: horse; "21"; golf; and around the world.

Offensive Scouting

If you are close to your opponents in ability, a sound scouting report and proper use of information can make the difference between victory and defeat. I firmly believe that scouting is a must at any level of play. It can help you upset a superior opponent, it will build morale and, most importantly, it will help you win games.

The following are our procedures for offensive basketball scouting:

1. If at all possible, scout the game yourself. You know your team's strengths and weaknesses better than anyone else.
2. If possible, get to the game early. Try to sit up as high in the bleachers as you can to get a clear view of the court.
3. During warm-up time, get the numbers of the players down and watch them shoot. Note their favorite spots for shooting.
4. Chart the "little things," such as out-of-bounds plays, both side and under, jump-ball formations, and anything special. Look for their offensive and defensive free-throw alignments.
5. Diagram the offensive and defensive setups.
6. Look for the weak spots in the defensive alignment.
7. At every time out, use the time to assess the opponent.
8. At half time, check your report to see if you have left anything out. Discuss the game with others.
9. During the second half, look for adjustments or anything new in the offensive or defensive alignments.
10. After the game is over, write up your report immediately, while scouting points are still fresh in your mind.

There are several types of charts that can be used for scouting or for your personal team statistics. The following are a few of the charts we use.

INDIVIDUAL SHOT CHART

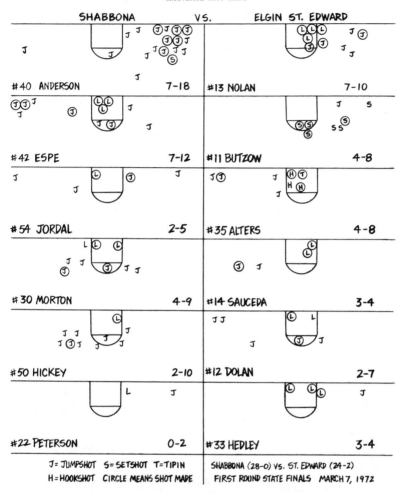

10-5

Diagram 10-5 is our Individual Shot Chart. Our statisticians keep individual and type-of-shot field-goal accuracy for each player in the game. Diagram 10-5 illustrates every shot taken by a St. Edward and Shabbona player in the first round of the state finals. The types of shots taken by the individual are denoted in the bottom left side of the chart.

For example, Nolan, for the game, made four layups in four tries, three jumpshots in six attempts, for a total of seven out of ten attempts.

Diagram 10-6 is one of our offensive scouting forms. The court diagrams are used for offensive patterns, jump-ball plays, offense versus press, defensive formation, etc. On the right is ample space for notes to be jotted down throughout the course of the game.

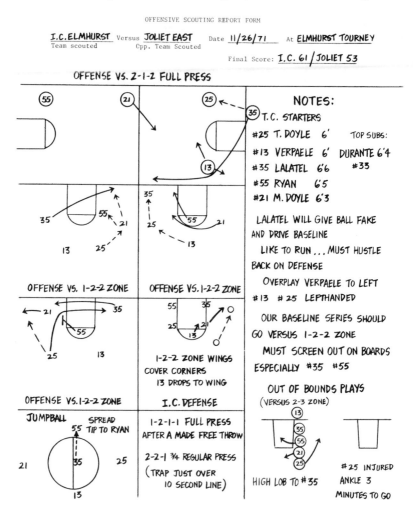

OFFENSIVE SCOUTING REPORT FORM

I.C. ELMHURST Versus JOLIET EAST   Date 11/26/71   At ELMHURST TOURNEY
Team scouted   Opp. Team Scouted

Final Score: I.C. 61 / JOLIET 53

OFFENSE VS. 2-1-2 FULL PRESS

NOTES:

T.C. STARTERS

#25 T. DOYLE 6'   TOP SUBS:
#13 VERPAELE 6'   DURANTE 6'4
#35 LALATEL 6'6   #33
#55 RYAN 6'5
#21 M. DOYLE 6'3

LALATEL WILL GIVE BALL FAKE
AND DRIVE BASELINE

LIKE TO RUN... MUST HUSTLE
BACK ON DEFENSE

OVERPLAY VERPAELE TO LEFT
#13 #25 LEFTHANDED

OUR BASELINE SERIES SHOULD
GO VERSUS 1-2-2 ZONE

MUST SCREEN OUT ON BOARDS
ESPECIALLY #35 #55

OFFENSE VS. 1-2-2 ZONE   OFFENSE VS. 1-2-2 ZONE

1-2-2 ZONE WINGS
COVER CORNERS
13 DROPS TO WING

OFFENSE VS. 1-2-2 ZONE   I.C. DEFENSE

JUMPBALL   SPREAD   1-2-1-1 FULL PRESS
55 TIP TO RYAN   AFTER A MADE FREE THROW

2-2-1 ¾ REGULAR PRESS
(TRAP JUST OVER
10 SECOND LINE)

OUT OF BOUNDS PLAYS
(VERSUS 2-3 ZONE)

HIGH LOB TO #35   #25 INJURED
                      ANKLE 3
                      MINUTES TO GO

10-6

Diagram 10-7 is our game-shot chart. The illustration lists the first-half scoring by us in our Sectional championship game with

GAME SHOT CHART

ELGIN ST. EDWARD VERSUS **HAMPSHIRE** SECTIONAL CHAMPIONSHIP GAME

Score at half **ELGIN 32/ HAMPSHIRE 18**

Date **MARCH 3, 1972**

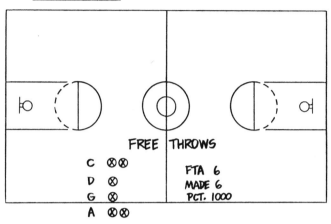

FREE THROWS

C ⊗⊗
D ⊗
G ⊗
A ⊗⊗

FTA 6
MADE 6
PCT. 1000

A. ALTERS
B. DOLAN
C. NOLAN
D. SAUCEDA
E. BUTZOW
F. HEDLEY
G. WAHL
H. PALUMBO
I. PAULIK
J. HANSEN

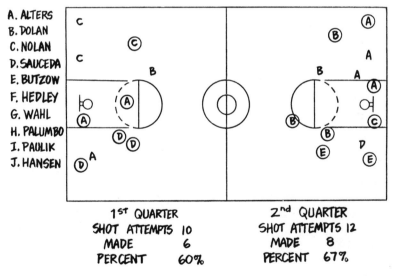

1ST QUARTER
SHOT ATTEMPTS 10
MADE 6
PERCENT 60%

2nd QUARTER
SHOT ATTEMPTS 12
MADE 8
PERCENT 67%

10-7

Hampshire High School. The free throws attempted and made by
each player are listed at the top of the chart. Each player's name is
given a letter, for instance, A is Alters, B is Dolan, C is Nolan, etc.

As depicted, we made six of six free throws the first half. At the bottom of the chart, the same letters are used to denote where on the court the field goals were made and by which player in the first quarter (at the left) and the second quarter (at the right). For example, in the first quarter Alters (A) made one of two field-goal attempts; Nolan (C) made one of three, Sauceda (D) made three of three, and Dolan (B) missed his only attempt.

Index